The Book of Tijani Litanies

Containing the Obligatory, Optional, and Special Litanies of the Tijāniyyah Ṭarīqah

TRANSLATED BY KAREEM MONIB AND SHUAIB KHAN

International Tijani Community Association

The Book of Tijani Litanies

Containing the Obligatory, Optional, and Special Litanies of the Tijāniyyah Ṭarīqah

Published by:
International Tijani Community Association
Embaba, Cairo, Egypt

Cover Design: Sherine Halim

Translation: Kareem Monib, Shuaib Khan

A CIP record for this book is acailable from the Library of Congress Cataloging-in-Publication Data

ISBN-13: 979-8-218-27858-8

Printed in USA

CONTENTS

Chapter 1

THE BLESSED LITANIES

The blessed litanies of the Tijānī Path are divided into three categories:

1. **Obligatory litanies** which become incumbent upon entering the Path. These are the daily *wird* (الوِرْد) and the weekly *haylalah* (الهَيْلَلَة).

2. **Optional litanies**. These include the *waẓīfah*[1] as well as everything that comes to us from the Messenger of Allah ﷺ and is contained in his pure and blessed Sunnah.

3. **Special litanies**. These are litanies (أَوْرَاد), remembrances (أَذْكَار), and beneficial phrases (فَوَائِد) that a *muqaddam*[2] gives certain deserving *murīds*[3] permission to recite.

Though these categories exist, the litanies of the Path have another dimension which is in fact more profound and vaster in scope than them. We call this greater dimension *love.* We recite these litanies because we have a love so great, it requires

1 The optionality of the *waẓīfah* is mentioned explicitly by Sīdī ʿAlī Ḥarāzim in *Jawāhir al-Maʿānī.*

2 A مُقَدَّم is someone authorized by the Shaykh of a *ṭarīqah* or spiritual path of Islam to transmit its litanies.

3 A مُرِيد is a seeker on the Path; namely, any person who has taken an oath to follow a Shaykh in the litanies and other teachings of one of the paths in Islam which are connected back to the Messsenger of Allah ﷺ by a validly-connected chain of transmission.

every atom in our being. The people of love are so immersed in the ocean of love that they do not differentiate between a litany that is obligatory and one that is optional or special. If we were to somehow come out of our spiritual intoxication only then could we start drawing distinctions. But that is nigh impossible as the lover is in perpetual union with the presence of his Beloved.

Chapter 2

THE OBLIGATORY LITANIES OF THE PATH

These are:

1. The daily *wird*.

2. The weekly *haylalah*.

The Daily Wird

The daily *wird* consists of reciting:

(100x) of asking forgivness from Allah by saying *astaghfiru Llāh* (أَسْتَغْفِرُ الله). This exact phrase must be used.

(100x) of asking Allah to send *ṣalāt* upon the Prophet ﷺ. Any formula of *ṣalāt* may be used, however it is best to use the prayer called *Ṣalāt al-Fātiḥ* (صَلَاةُ الفَاتِح).[4] One should continue with whatever formula one began with until completing the hundred.

(100x) of the statement of Divine oneness: *la ilāha illā Llāh* (لا إِلٰهَ إلا الله). This exact phrase must be used.

The *wird* is recited twice every day, once in the morning and once in the evening.

Some rules regarding the daily *wird*:

1. Each recital has an open period (إِخْتِيَارِي) during which time one can choose to recite the *wird* at any point of time in that period; as well as an urgent period (ضَرُورِي) during which one should not delay reciting the *wird* without necessity.

The open period for the morning recital is from the time of the morning prayer (i.e. after one prays the morning prayer) until just before noon. The urgent period is from just before noon until sunset.

The open period for the evening recital is from the afternoon or *ʿaṣr* prayer until the evening or *ʿishāʾ* prayer. Its

4 The exact wording of this prayer, along with the tranliteration and translation are included in a separate chapter of this book for ease of reference.

urgent time is from the evening until dawn.

The best time to recite the *wird* is during its open period. If one fails to recite the *wird* during its urgent period, then one has missed its time of performance and must make it up.

2. One is allowed to say the morning *wird* earlier in the night and this does not have to be out of necessity. In fact, it is recommended to do so because the reward for one recitation of *Ṣalāt al-Fātiḥ* at night is multiples of the reward one recieves during the day. One can recite it early starting at a time after the *'ishā'* prayer equal to the time it takes to recite five *ḥizbs*[5] of the Quran. This applies to the time period between the *'ishā'* prayer and *fajr* (dawn) prayer. If the fajr prayer arrives before completing the *wird*, one finishes the *wird* and does not repeat it.

3. One cannot recite the evening *wird* earlier than its appointed time except for a reason outside of one's control in which case one says the morning *wird* first and then the evening *wird* after it.

4. The *wird* is rendered invalid by eating or drinking while reciting it even if the amount is small.

5. Laughing audibly also invalidates the *wird*.

6. If one is riding a car or train, one is allowed to recite the *wird* right where one is seated if one's shoes are ritually clean.[6] If they are not, one should remove them and place one's feet on top of them, being careful to not move one's feet around while saying the *wird*. One should also make sure one's seat is ritually clean.

---

5 A حِزْب (plural أَحْزَاب) is equal to 1/60th of the Quran or half of a *juz'*.

6 Clean here translates طَاهِر which refers to ritual cleanliness and not ordinary cleanliness. It means to be pure of those things consider filthy in the revealed law, things such as the urine or feces of animals we do not eat.

7. The sick, as well as women in their menstrual period or experiencing post-partum bleeding, are not obligated to recite the *wird*, but may choose to do so.

8. If, while reciting the *wird*, one begins to doubt the number of times one has recited a given formula, one should continue from the last number one was sure of and then recite *ashtaghfiru Llāh* one hundred times at the completion of the *wird*.

9. One may, out of necessity, begin the second part of the *wird* with *Ṣalāt al-Fātiḥ* and complete it with another form of *ṣalāt* on the Prophet ﷺ.

10. If one discovers that their prayer beads are missing some beads, then one only needs to make up the last *wird* that one recited.

11. If one is reciting the *wird*, and the time for the *haylalah* arrives and there is a group present to recite it, then one should complete their *wird* and then join them. However, if one's participation is necessary in order to have the requisite number for a group, then one should stop reciting the *wird* and join them right away.

12. If one is reciting the *wird* and comes across some people reciting the *waẓīfah*, then one should complete their *wird* and then join them. This applies even if one knows that one will not finish the *wird* in time to join them.

13. If one is reciting the *wird*, and the Imam ascends the pulpit for the Friday prayer, one should still complete their *wird*.

14. If one drops their prayer beads while reciting the *wird* and does not know the number that was recited of a given formula, then one should make their best estimate and resume, but if one prefers, one can start again from the beginning.

15. If one finishes reciting the *wird* and then subsequently finds some ritual impurity on their clothing, one does not need to repeat the *wird*. In the case where one notices ritual impurity while reciting the *wird*, there are further considerations. If the impurity is dry and easily removed then one should remove it and finish the *wird*. If it is not easily removed, then one should wash it off and repeat the *wird* from the beginning. This is true unless one is reciting during the urgent time period and there is just enough time remaining to finish the *wird*, then one should finish the *wird* even with the impurity on them. Finishing the *wird* in its appointed time takes precedence over being in a state of ritual purity while reciting it.

16. One must be in a state of *wuḍūʾ* and have a specific intention or *niyyah* for the *wird*. One must cover the requisite parts of the body, i.e. one's *ʿawrah*. One should not speak during the *wird*, from beginning to end, unless out of necessity in which case one should try to communicate by gesture first, and if that is not effective then one should try to use only one or two words at most. This applies to everyone except one's father, mother, or husband: for these, it is permissible to talk to them until they are satisfied and then resume where one left off, unless alot of talk transpires in which case one should start again from the beginning of the *wird*.

17. It is obligatory to return the greetings of someone who greets you with *as-salāmu alaykum*, either by speech or by gesture. While reciting the *wird*, it is recommended (مُسْتَحَب) to ask for mercy for one who sneezes and to repeat after the caller of the *adhān*.

18. It is permissible to recite the *wird* while having a small amount of impurity on oneself that is excusable. This amount is equal to a coin's size of blood, puss, or other ritual impurities.

19. If one forgets if one has recited the *wird* or not, one should repeat it. If one is unsure if one has recited a formu-

la the correct number of times, one resumes from the least number of the numbers that one is unsure about.

20. Reciting the *wird* consistently is considered the same as keeping an oath that one has made according to the revealed law. If one leaves it off or neglects it, one should seek a renewal of permission for it from a *muqaddam*.

The Weekly Haylalah

The weekly *haylalah* consists of reciting *la ilāha illā Llāh* (لا إله إلا الله) or the Divine name (الله). One may also mix betwen the two. The *haylalah* is recited after *ʿasr* prayer on Fridays, about an hour before sunset. One may cling to a specific number, between 1000 and 1600, or more if one wishes. In any case, one should recite the *haylalah* up until sunset. There are various opinions regarding the minimum number of times one should use, but these can be reconciled by saying that the minimum is 1000 for an individual and 300 for a group.

The Messenger of Allah ﷺ is present during the *haylalah* from its beginning to its end.

Friday was chosen as the day for the *haylalah* for the following reasons:

- In the heavenly realm, Friday is called the *Day of Increase*.
- It has been narrated in authenticated hadith that the False Messiah or *Dajjāl* will emerge on a Friday after *ʿaṣr* at which time all of the beloveds[7] (أَحْبَاب) will have congregated in the *zāwiyah*s reciting the *haylalah* and will not fall prey to him.

7 The term "beloveds" or *aḥbāb* is often used for the *murīds* in a Sufi path because of the love that exists between them and because of the Divine love that they aspire to attain.

- It has been narrated by many of our pious ancestors, including the famous four *ʿAbd Allah*s[8], that the hour of Divine acceptance[9] on Fridays is the hour immediately before sunset. It has also been narrated that the Prophet ﷺ said that Allah the Exalted said, ***"Whoever's remembrance of Me keeps him from asking things of Me, I will give him better than what can be asked for."***[10]
- Our actions are presented to Allah at this hour on Fridays. Thus, by performing the *haylalah*, the last thing written in the scroll of our weekly actions will be لا إله إلا الله and the first thing in our scroll will be لا إله إلا الله, and thus everthing in between will be forgiven.

Some rules regarding the *haylalah*:

1. If one misses the *haylalah*, it is not to be made up. However, if one misses it and wishes to nevertheless attain its merit, he or she should recite 500 *Ṣalat al-Fātiḥ* as has been transmitted by a number of great companions of the Shakyh ﷺ.

2. If one has a valid excuse and is unable to recite the *haylalah* up to sunset, the he or she is allowed ot recite the requisite number after *ʿaṣr* prayer and return to work.

3. The conditions for the *haylalah* include being in a group, reciting it aloud, and sitting in a circle, in rows, or in a rectanglur formation.

---

8 These are ʿAbd Allah b. ʿUmar ﷺ, ʿAbd Allah b. ʿAbbās ﷺ, ʿAbd Allah b. al-Zubayr ﷺ, and ʿAbd Allah b. ʿAmr b. al-ʿĀṣ ﷺ.

9 Abu Hurayrah ﷺ narrates that the Messenger of Allah ﷺ said, "There is an hour on Friday during which, if any Muslim stands and prays, asking for something good from Allah, then Allah will give it to him." Narrated in Bukhārī. قَالَ أَبُو الْقَاسِمِ صَلَّى اللهُ عَلَيْهِ وَسَلَّمَ : فِي الْجُمُعَةِ سَاعَةٌ لَا يُوَافِقُهَا عَبْدٌ مُسْلِمٌ قَائِمٌ يُصَلِّي فَسَأَلَ اللهَ خَيْرًا إِلَّا أَعْطَاهُ

10 Narrated by al-Bukhāri in his *Tārīkh* and in *Khalq Afʿāl al-ʿIbād* from Mālik b. al-Ḥārith ﷺ.

4. Women should not recite the *haylalah*, or the *waẓīfah* aloud, unless it is a women-only gathering in which case it is permitted to raise the voice slightly.

5. If a people in a given locality willfully neglect the *haylalah*, then they are taking serious matters lightly, and are all liable to losing permission in the Path - God forbid!

Chapter 3

THE OPTIONAL LITANY: THE *WAẒĪFAH*

The *waẓīfah* has three levels for recitation. Each one is considered complete in and of itself. These levels are:

1. The long (الطَويلَة) *waẓīfah*.
2. The short (الخَفيفَة) *waẓīfah*.
3. The light (الأَخَف) *waẓīfah*.

The Long Waẓīfah

The long version consists of the following:

(100x) of asking forgivness from Allah by saying *astaghfiru Llāh* (أَسْتَغْفِرُ الله).

(100x) of *Ṣalāt al-Fātiḥ* (صَلَاةُ الفَاتِح).

(200x) of the statement of Divine oneness: *la ilāha illā Llāh* (لا إله إلا الله).

(11x) of the prayer known as *Jawharat al-Kamāl*[11] (جَوْهَرَةُ الكَمَال).

The Short Waẓīfah

The short version consists of the following:

(30x) of asking forgivness from Allah by saying *astaghfiru Llāha l-'Adhīma lladhī lā ilāha illā huwa l-Ḥayya l-Qayyūm* (أَسْتَغْفِرُ اللهَ العَظِيمَ الَّذِي لَا إِلٰهَ إِلَّا هُوَ الحَيَّ القَيُّوم).[12]

(50x) of *Ṣalāt al-Fātiḥ* (صَلَاةُ الفَاتِح).

(100x) of the statement of Divine oneness: *la ilāha illā Llāh* (لا إله إلا الله).

(11x) of the prayer known as *Jawharat al-Kamāl*[13] (جَوْهَرَةُ الكَمَال).

---

11 The exact wording of this prayer, along with the tranliteration and translation are included in a separate chapter of this book for ease of reference.

12 "I ask forgiveness from Allah the Magnificent, other than whom there is no god, the Alive, the Self-Subsisting."

13 The exact wording of this prayer, along with the tranliteration and translation are included in a separate chapter of this book for ease of reference.

The Light Waẓīfah

The lightest version consists of the following:

(10x) of asking forgivness from Allah by saying *astaghfiru Llāha l-ʿAdhīma lladhī lā ilāha illā huwa l-Ḥayya l-Qayyūma wa atūbu ilayh* (أَسْتَغْفِرُ اللهَ العَظِيمَ الَّذِي لَا إِلٰهَ إِلَّا هُوَ الحَيَّ القَيُّومَ وَأَتُوبُ إِلَيْهِ).[14]

(20x) of *Ṣalāt al-Fātiḥ* (صَلَاةُ الفَاتِح).

(50x) of the statement of Divine oneness: *la ilāha illā Llāh* (لا إله إلا الله).

(7x) of the prayer known as *Jawharat al-Kamāl* (جَوْهَرَةُ الكَمَال).

Some rules pertaining to reciting the *waẓīfah*:

1. The *waẓīfah* has optional timings. It can be recited twice, once in the morning and once in the evening. It can also be recited only once a day. There is no specific time in the day that it should be recited, rather it is up to the murīd as to when they prefer to recite it each day. For example, one can recite it in the morning one day, in the evening the next, and at noon the following day, etc.

2. If one has not memorized the prayer called *Jawharat al-Kamāl*, then he or she can recite 20 *Ṣalāt al-Fātiḥ* in its place if one is reciting the long or short version of the *waẓīfah*; or 10 *Ṣalāt al-Fātiḥ* in its place if one is reciting the light version of the *waẓīfah*.

3. If one joins the *waẓīfah* late, one should join the group wherever they are in the recitation. When they are finished,

---

14 ***"I ask forgiveness from Allah the Magnificent, other than whom there is no god, the Alive, the Self-Subsisting; and I repent to Him."*** This version of asking forgiveness is narrated in the hadith by Abu Dawūd and al-Tirmidhī with a good (جَيِّد) chain of transmission.

then one should make up the portions that one missed, in order, starting with *astaghfiru Llāh* and without saying the *Basmalah* or *Surat al-Fātiḥah,*[15] because those entry-words are recommended for those who are at the opening of the *waẓīfah*.

4. If someone makes a mistake like saying the parts of the *waẓīfah* out of order, then one should treat the part that was said out of order as if it has not been recited, and assume that one has only recited the portion that was in the correct order. For example, if one said the *haylalah* (لا إلٰه إلا الله) before the prayers upon the Prophet ﷺ, then one would treat the *haylalah* as if it had not been recited, and one would resume with the correct order starting from after the *istighfār*. After this, one should recite *astaghfiru Llāh* (100x) to rectify the mistake (unless one is in a group in which case there is no need to recite the *istighfār* to rectify the mistake). This rectification of the *waẓīfah* - by reciting the *istighfār* - is obligatory; if one willfully neglects it, the *waẓīfah* is considered to not have been performed.

5. If a group makes a mistake or forgets something from the *waẓīfah*, they can simply recite what was missed after they complete it, and rectification of the mistake by reciting the *istighfār* is not necessary.

6. The *waẓīfah* is rendered un-performed if one eats or drinks while reciting it.

7. It is not obligatory to make up a missed *waẓīfah* if an entire day has passed and one has not recited it.

8. If one has already recited the *waẓīfah* in a group and then goes to visit some Tijānies who happen to be reciting the *waẓīfah* together, then one can join their group but should not make-up any missed portions of the *waẓīfah*. This is because one has joined the second group based on the

15 It is customary to say certain "entry-words" called a *maqṣad* before starting the litanies.

Prophetic tradition: "***If you pass by the gardens of Paradise, then relax therein.***"[16]

9. One can recite the *Jawharat al-Kamāl* prayer while walking, riding in vehicle, or sitting, as long as one feels fairly certain the place is clean.

10. One can recite the *Jawharat al-Kamāl* prayer outside of the *waẓīfah* without *wuḍū'*. However, in the *waẓīfah*, one must be in ritual purity, either by using water or dirt (i.e. *tayammum*).

16 Narrated by Ahmad, al-Bayhaqī, Abū Yaʿlā, Abū Nuʿaym, Ibn ʿAsākir in his *Tārīkh* from Anas ﷺ. Narrated by Tirmidhī, who said it is *ḥasan*, from Abū Hurayrah ﷺ. al-Ṭabarānī narrates it in *al-Kabīr* from Ibn ʿAbbās ﷺ.

Chapter 4

MAQĀṢID: ENTRY AND CLOSURE WORDS

Maqāṣid are optional words that one may recite before, during, or at the closing of the litanies. For easy reference of the entire *wird*, incuding the entry and closure words, please see relevant chapter at the end of this book.

Maqāṣid of the Wird

- **Before the** *wird*, one recites *Ṣūrat al-Fātiḥah:*

بِسْمِ اللَّهِ الرَّحْمَٰنِ الرَّحِيمِ ﴿١﴾ الْحَمْدُ لِلَّهِ رَبِّ الْعَالَمِينَ ﴿٢﴾ الرَّحْمَٰنِ
الرَّحِيمِ ﴿٣﴾ مَالِكِ يَوْمِ الدِّينِ ﴿٤﴾ إِيَّاكَ نَعْبُدُ وَإِيَّاكَ نَسْتَعِينُ ﴿٥﴾ اهْدِنَا
الصِّرَاطَ الْمُسْتَقِيمَ ﴿٦﴾ صِرَاطَ الَّذِينَ أَنْعَمْتَ عَلَيْهِمْ غَيْرِ الْمَغْضُوبِ
عَلَيْهِمْ وَلَا الضَّالِّينَ ﴿٧﴾ آمِين

bismillāhir-raḥmānir-raḥīmil-ḥamdu lillāhi rabbil-ʿālamīn, ar-raḥmānir-raḥīm, māliki yawmid-dīn. iyyāka naʿbudu wa iyyāka nastaʿīn. ihdinaṣ-ṣirāṭal-mustaqīm, ṣirāṭal-ladhīna anʿamta ʿalayhim, ghayril-maghḍūbi ʿalayhim wa laḍ-ḍālīn. āmīn.

and then *Ṣalāt al-Fātiḥ:*

اللّهُمَّ صَلِّ وَسَلِّمْ عَلَىٰ سَيِّدِنَا مُحَمَّدٍ الفَاتِحِ لِمَا أُغْلِقَ والخَاتِمِ لِمَا سَبَقَ نَاصِرِ الحَقِّ بِالحَقِّ والهَادِي إِلَىٰ صِراطِكَ المُسْتَقِيمِ وعَلَىٰ آلِهِ حَقَّ قَدْرِكَ وَمِقْدَارِكَ العَظِيمِ

Allāhumma ṣalli wa sallim ʿalā sayyidinā muḥammad-inil-fātiḥi limā ughliqa, wal-khātimi limā sabaqa, nāṣiril-ḥaqqi bil-haqqi, wal-hādī ilā ṣirāṭikal-mustaqīm, wa ʿalā ālihi haqqa qadrika wa miqdārikal-ʿaẓīm.

and then:

سُبْحَانَ رَبِّكَ رَبِّ الْعِزَّةِ عَمَّا يَصِفُونَ ۝ وَسَلَامٌ عَلَى الْمُرْسَلِينَ ۝ وَالْحَمْدُ لِلهِ رَبِّ الْعَالَمِينَ ۝

subḥāna rabbika rabbil-ʿizzati ʿammā yaṣifūn, wa salāmun ʿalal-mursalīn, wal-ḥamdu lillāhi rabbil-ʿālamīn.

- **During the** *wird*, after reciting *Ṣalāt al-Fātiḥ*, recite:

سُبْحَانَ رَبِّكَ رَبِّ الْعِزَّةِ عَمَّا يَصِفُونَ ۝ وَسَلَامٌ عَلَى الْمُرْسَلِينَ ۝ وَالْحَمْدُ لِلهِ رَبِّ الْعَالَمِينَ ۝

subḥāna rabbika rabbil-ʿizzati ʿammā yaṣifūn, wa salāmun ʿalal-mursalīn, wal-ḥamdu lillāhi rabbil-ʿālamīn

- **At the end of the** *wird*, recite:

سَيِّدِنَا مُحَمَّدٌ رَسُولُ اللهِ ۝ عَلَيْهِ سَلَامُ اللهِ

sayyidunā muḥammadur-rasūlul-lāh, ʿalayhi salāmul-lāh

And then:

إِنَّ اللَّهَ وَمَلَائِكَتَهُ يُصَلُّونَ عَلَى النَّبِيِّ ۚ يَا أَيُّهَا الَّذِينَ آمَنُوا صَلُّوا عَلَيْهِ وَسَلِّمُوا تَسْلِيمًا

inna-llāha wa malā'ikatahu yuṣallūna ʿalan-nabiyy. yā ayyu-hal-ladhīna āmanū ṣallū ʿalayhi wa sallimū taslīmā

And then one should ask Allah for whatever one wishes to ask (*duʿā'*).

And then, one should recite *Ṣūrat al-Fātiḥah:*

بِسْمِ اللَّهِ الرَّحْمَٰنِ الرَّحِيمِ ۝١ الْحَمْدُ لِلَّهِ رَبِّ الْعَالَمِينَ ۝٢ الرَّحْمَٰنِ الرَّحِيمِ ۝٣ مَالِكِ يَوْمِ الدِّينِ ۝٤ إِيَّاكَ نَعْبُدُ وَإِيَّاكَ نَسْتَعِينُ ۝٥ اهْدِنَا الصِّرَاطَ الْمُسْتَقِيمَ ۝٦ صِرَاطَ الَّذِينَ أَنْعَمْتَ عَلَيْهِمْ غَيْرِ الْمَغْضُوبِ عَلَيْهِمْ وَلَا الضَّالِّينَ ۝٧ آمِين

bismillāhir-raḥmānir-raḥīmil-ḥamdu lillāhi rabbil-ʿālamīn, ar-raḥmānir-raḥīm, māliki yawmid-dīn. iyyāka naʿbudu wa iyyāka nastaʿīn. ihdinaṣ-ṣirāṭal-mustaqīm, ṣirāṭal-ladhīna anʿamta ʿalayhim, ghayril-maghḍūbi ʿalayhim wa laḍ-ḍālīn. āmīn.

And then recite:

سُبْحَانَ رَبِّكَ رَبِّ الْعِزَّةِ عَمَّا يَصِفُونَ ۝ وَسَلَامٌ عَلَى الْمُرْسَلِينَ ۝ وَالْحَمْدُ للهِ رَبِّ الْعَالَمِينَ ۝

subḥāna rabbika rabbil-ʿizzati ʿammā yaṣifūn, wa salāmun ʿalal-mursalīn, wal-ḥamdu lillāhi rabbil-ʿālamīn

And then recite:

إِنَّ اللَّهَ وَمَلَائِكَتَهُ يُصَلُّونَ عَلَى النَّبِيِّ ۚ يَا أَيُّهَا الَّذِينَ آمَنُوا صَلُّوا عَلَيْهِ وَسَلِّمُوا تَسْلِيمًا

inna-llāha wa malā'ikatahu yuṣallūna ʿalan-nabiyy. yā ayyuhal-ladhīna āmanū ṣallū ʿalayhi wa sallimū taslīmā

Maqāṣid of the Haylalah

- **Before the** *haylalah*, one recites the same entry words as before the *wird.*
- **After the** *haylalah*, one recites the same closure words as after the *wird.*

Maqāṣid of the Waẓīfah

- **Before the** *waẓīfah*, one recites *Ṣūrat al-Fātiḥah:*

بِسْمِ اللَّهِ الرَّحْمَٰنِ الرَّحِيمِ ﴿١﴾ الْحَمْدُ لِلَّهِ رَبِّ الْعَالَمِينَ ﴿٢﴾ الرَّحْمَٰنِ الرَّحِيمِ ﴿٣﴾ مَالِكِ يَوْمِ الدِّينِ ﴿٤﴾ إِيَّاكَ نَعْبُدُ وَإِيَّاكَ نَسْتَعِينُ ﴿٥﴾ اهْدِنَا الصِّرَاطَ الْمُسْتَقِيمَ ﴿٦﴾ صِرَاطَ الَّذِينَ أَنْعَمْتَ عَلَيْهِمْ غَيْرِ الْمَغْضُوبِ عَلَيْهِمْ وَلَا الضَّالِّينَ ﴿٧﴾ آمين

bismillāhir-raḥmānir-raḥīmil-ḥamdu lillāhi rabbil-ʿālamīn, ar-raḥmānir-raḥīm, māliki yawmid-dīn. iyyāka naʿbudu wa iyyāka nastaʿīn. ihdinaṣ-ṣirāṭal-mustaqīm, ṣirāṭal-ladhīna anʿamta ʿalayhim, ghayril-maghḍūbi ʿalayhim wa laḍ-ḍālīn. āmīn.

- **After one recites the *Ṣalāt al-Fātiḥ* portion**, one recites:

سُبْحَانَ رَبِّكَ رَبِّ الْعِزَّةِ عَمَّا يَصِفُونَ ۝ وَسَلَامٌ عَلَى الْمُرْسَلِينَ ۝ وَالْحَمْدُ لِلَّهِ رَبِّ الْعَالَمِينَ ۝

subḥāna rabbika rabbil-ʿizzati ʿammā yaṣifūn, wa salāmun ʿalal-mursalīn, wal-ḥamdu lillāhi rabbil-ʿālamīn

- **After the** *waẓīfah*, one recites:

إِنَّ اللَّهَ وَمَلَائِكَتَهُ يُصَلُّونَ عَلَى النَّبِيِّ ۚ يَا أَيُّهَا الَّذِينَ آمَنُوا صَلُّوا عَلَيْهِ وَسَلِّمُوا تَسْلِيمًا

inna-llāha wa malā'ikatahu yuṣallūna 'alan-nabiyy. yā ayyu-hal-ladhīna āmanū ṣallū 'alayhi wa sallimū taslīmā

And finally, one recites:

سُبْحَانَ رَبِّكَ رَبِّ الْعِزَّةِ عَمَّا يَصِفُونَ ۝ وَسَلَامٌ عَلَى الْمُرْسَلِينَ ۝
وَالْحَمْدُ لِلّٰهِ رَبِّ الْعَالَمِينَ ۝

subḥāna rabbika rabbil-'izzati 'ammā yaṣifūn, wa salāmun 'alal-mursalīn, wal-ḥamdu lillāhi rabbil-'ālamīn

Chapter 5

MISCELLANEOUS MATTERS

1. One is encouraged to gift the reward of all of one's litanies to the blessed presence of the Messenger of Allah ﷺ on behalf of the Shaykh, while bearing a firm conviction that the Prophet ﷺ has no need of our gift because Allah has enriched him as He says, ***"Verily, your Lord will give you until you are satisfied."***[17] The truth is that everything we do is already written in his ﷺ book of good deeds, because he is the source of these practices and the one who taught them to us. Our gifting here is simply an expression of our love and nothing else. Indeed, the wont of the great ones is to give all of their actions to him ﷺ, both the obligatory and devotional; they do this because they see all of their actions to be on his behalf ﷺ.

2. Sidi Ahmad Tijani said, "One should not pray behind anyone who hates the Shaykh, because the imam is an intercessor, and how can one take a man as an intercessor who hates his Shaykh? To do so would be to take them as a friend and protector, something which is contrary to sound nature."

3. Know that after true love for the Shaykh enters the

17 Quran al-Ḍuḥā: 5

heart a *murīd*; after his connection to the rope of the Path grows stronger; after he is sure that he would never become attached to another shaykh, nor would he ever seek the spritual help of other *awliyā'*, may Allah sanctify their secrets, whether alive or dead - not even if he came across the Quṭb of the Age and saw marvelous miracles indicating his great saintly rank; if a *murīd* is sure of all this, then he may visit any of the *awliyā'* he wishes without harm. He can visit their graves, and sit there, and greet them. He can seek to learn more about their virtues and works.

4. The use of esoteric practices (أَسْرَار), talismans, letterology, and other similar things was expressly and strictly prohibited by the Shaykh. There are reports that Sidi Ahmad Tijani used such things at the beginning of his path, but that when he saw the Messenger of Allah ﷺ, he had no need of such things, having recieved much greater than that from the Prophet ﷺ himself who also commanded him to spend his time reciting *Ṣalāt al-Fātiḥ* and the Great Name, each at their various levels.

5. If one sees the Shaykh in a dream or in the waking state and is commanded to practice a specific *dhikr* or litany; or a *dhikr* from another path; or one is given permission to transmit the *wird* to whoever asks for it, then the permission one received in this vision is valid. One does not, in this case, need to get permission from a *muqaddam* or anyone else and he can transmit those litanies he has reeeived permission for whether they are general litanies or special ones.

6. The Shaykh would always recite the Verse of the Throne (آيَةُ الكُرْسِي) in the first cycle (رَكْعَة) of the morning prayer (صَلَاةُ الصُّبْح) and would recite *Ṣūrat al-Qadr* in the second cycle. He maintained this practice until he died. He would also say the follwoing *dhikr* in the first prostration of the morning prayer: *subḥān Allāhi wa l-ḥamdu li Llāhi wa lā ilāha illa Llāhu wa Llāhu akbar wa lā ḥawla wa lā quwwata illā bi Llāhi mil'a mā 'alima wa 'adada mā 'alima wa zinata*

mā ʿalima - once according to one narration and three times in another; and then in the second prostration he would recite *Ṣalāt al-Fātiḥ* one or three times. It is also reported that he would both make *duʿāʾ* and recite *Ṣalāt al-Fātiḥ* in each prostration.

Chapter 6

صِلاةُ الفَاتِحِ
ṢALĀT AL-FĀTIḤ

اللّٰهُمَّ صَلِّ وَسَلِّمْ عَلَىٰ سَيِّدِنَا مُحَمَّدٍ الفَاتِحِ لِمَا أُغْلِقَ والخَاتِمِ لِمَا سَبَقَ نَاصِرِ الحَقِّ بِالحَقِّ والهَادِي إِلَىٰ صِرَاطِكَ المُسْتَقِيمِ وعَلَىٰ آلِهِ حَقَّ قَدْرِكَ وَمِقْدَارِكَ العَظِيمِ

Allāhumma ṣalli wa sallim ʿalā sayyidinā Muḥammadini ʿl-fātiḥi limā uġliqa wal khātimi limā sabaqa nāṣiri ʿl-ḥaqqi bi ʿl-ḥaqqi wa ʿl-hādi ʿilā ṣirātika ʿl-mustaqīm wa ʿalā ālihi ḥaqqa qadrika wa miqdārika ʿl-ʿaẓīm

O Allah, send *ṣalawåt* on our master Muhammad, the opener of what was closed, and the sealer of what went before; the helper of the Truth by the Truth, and the guide to Your straight path; and on his family, - as is due Your immense esteem and grandeur.

Chapter 7

جوهرة الكمال
JAWHARAT AL-KAMĀL

اللَّهُمَّ صَلِّ وَسَلِّمْ عَلي عَيْنِ الرَّحْمَةِ الرَّبَّانِيَّةِ وَالْياقوتَةِ الْمُتحَقِّقَةِ الْحائِطَةِ بِمَرْكَزِ الْفُهومِ وَالْمَعاني وَنورِ الْأَكْوانِ الْمُتَكَوِّنَةِ الْآدَمِيِّ صاحِبِ الْحَقِّ الرَّبَّاني الْبَرْقِ الْأَسْطَعِ بِمُزونِ الْأَرْباحِ الْمالِئَةِ لِكُلِّ مُتَعَرِّضٍ مِنَ الْبُحورِ وَالْأَواني وَنورِكَ اللَّامِعِ الَّذي مَلَأْتَ بِهِ كَوْنَكَ الْمَكْنونِ في السَّبْعِ الْمَثاني اللَّهُمَّ صَلِّ وَسَلِّمْ عَلي عَيْنِ الْحَقِّ الَّتي تَتَجَلَّي مِنْها عُروشُ الْحَقائِقِ عَيْنِ الْمَعارِفِ الْأَكْرَم صِراطِكَ التَّامِّ الْأَقْوَم اللَّهُمَّ صَلِّ وَسَلِّمْ عَلي طَلْعَةِ الْحَقِّ بِالْحَقِّ الْكَنْزِ الْأَعْظَمِ إِفاضَتِكَ مِنْكَ إِلَيْكَ إِحاطَةِ النُّورِ الْمُطَلْسَمِ صَلَّي اللهُ عَلَيْهِ وَعَلي آلِهِ صَلاةً تُعَرِّفُنا بِها إِيَّاه

Allāhumma ṣalli wa sallim ʿalā ʿayni r-raḥmati r-rabbāniyyati wa l-yāqūtati l-mutaḥaqqiqati l-ḥāʾiṭati bi markazi l-fuhūmi wa l-maʿānī wa nūri l-akwāni l-mutakawwinati l-ādamiyyi ṣāḥibi l-ḥaqqi r-rabbānī al-barqi l-asṭaʿi bi muzūni l-arbāḥi l-māliʾati li kulli mutaʿarriḍin mina l-buḥūri wa l-awānī wa nūrika l-lāmiʾ l-ladhī malaʾta bihi kawnaka l-maknūni fi s-sabʿi l-mathānī. Allāhumma ṣalli wa sallim ʿalā ʿayni l-ḥaqqi llatī tatajallā minhā ʿurūshu l-ḥaqāʾiq ʿayni l-maʿārifi l-akram ṣirāṭika t-tāmmi l-aqwam. Allāhumma ṣalli wa sallim ʿalā ṭalʿati l-ḥaqqi bi l-ḥaqqi l-kanzi l-aʿẓam ifāḍatika minka ilayka iḥāṭati n-nūri l-muṭalsam Ṣalla Llāhu ʿalayhi wa ʿalā ālihi ṣalātan tuʿarrifunā bihā iyyāh

O Allah send *ṣalāt* and *salām* on the fount of lordly mercy. The true emerald encompassing the center of all comprehensions and meanings; the light of the worlds that comprise the Adamite, the possessor of the lordly right; the most brilliant lightning in the rain-laden clouds of goodly gains that fill every receptacle among oceans and vessels; and your radiant light with which you filled Your universe and which is hidden in your seven oft-repeated verses. O Allah, send *ṣalāt* and *salām* on the fount of the Real, from which the thrones of realities are manifested; the fount of the most noble knowledge, Your most complete and straightest path. O Allah, send *ṣalāt* and *salām* on the appearance of the Real through the Real, the greatest treasure; Your outpouring, from You to You, the encompassment of the hidden light. Send *ṣalāt* upon him and his family, a *ṣalāt* by which You will make him known to us.

Chapter 8

SPECIAL LITANIES

We present these special litanies (الأَوْرادُ الخَاصَّة) here because there are no secrets between beloveds and because these litanies are self-protecting in the sense that no one can maintain their regular practice except those who are fit for them.

I have given all Tijani's in the East and West permission to select from these litanies whichever they are comfortable with.

-Salaheldin al-Tijani al-Hassani

الفَاتِحَةُ بِنِيَّةِ الإِسْمِ الأَعْظَمِ

Al-Fātiḥah with the intention of the Greatest Name

Sidi Ahmad al-Tijani ﷺ said, "One recitation of *al-Fātiḥah*[18] with the intention of the Greatest Name (الإِسْمُ الأَعْظَم) equals 4,000,000,000,000 of *Ṣalāt al-Fātiḥ*."

This is the greatest *dhikr* that exists for *al-Fātiḥah* contains the Greatest Name of Allah.

The conditions for the validity of this *dhikr* is as follows:

1. Valid permission, specifically for reciting it on behalf of the Shaykh (النِيَابَة). This is a specific permission that is not included in general permissions (مُطْلَق الإِذْن).

2. The intention for reciting the Greatest Name should be brought into the heart.

3. One must recite on behalf of our master Sidi Ahmad al-Tijani ﷺ. This means that the remembrancer recites it as if Shaykh al-Tijani is the one reciting it; one thus recieves the lights and secrets of the Tijani tongue in one's *dhikr*.

4. One must be in a state of ritual purity using water (الطَهَارَةُ المَائِيَّة). *Tayammum* does not suffice.

5. The place where one sits must be clean from any ritual impurities.

6. One's body and clothes must also be clean from any ritual impurities.

7. This *dhikr* should be recited between the morning

---

18 The first chapter of the Quran.

prayer (صَلَاةُ الصُّبح) and sunrise, or else between the afternoon prayer (صَلَاةُ العَصْر) and sunset.

8. One should choose one of the following numbers of repetitions and maintain it: 7 or 9 or 33 or 77 or 99. If one accidentally recites it 100 times, then one should rectify the mistake by reciting *Ṣalāt al-Fātiḥ* 1000 times. The largest number for this *dhikr* is 99 and no more.

The conditions for perfection of this *dhikr* are as follows:

1. Gifting its reward to the presence of the Messenger of Allah ﷺ.

2. Facing the *qiblah.*

3. It should be recited after the obligatory morning *wird* (for those say it after *fajr* prayer).

4. One should connect the letter *mīm* at the end of the *Basmalah* to the beginning of the *Ḥamdalah* in one continuous breath.[19]

5. One should recite the following *maqṣad*:

اللَّهُمَّ إِنِّي نَوَيْتُ تِلَاوَةَ اسْمِكَ العَظِيمِ الأَعْظَمِ الكَبِيرِ الأَكْبَرِ بِتَلَاوَةِ الفَاتِحَةِ - وتُحَدِّدْ العَدَدَ[20] - بِنِيَّةِ إِهْدَاءِ ثَوَابِهَا إِلَي سَيِّدِ الوُجُودِ وَعَلَمِ الشُّهُود سَيِّدِنَا مُحَمَّدٍ صَلَّي اللهُ عَلَيْهِ وَسَلَّمَ وَنِيَابَةً عَنْ شَيْخِنَا وَوَسِيلَتِنَا إِلَي رَبِّنَا سِيدي أَبِي العَبَّاسِ أَحْمَدَ بْنِ مُحَمَّدٍ التِّجَانِي رَضِيَ اللهُ عَنْهُ وَأَقُولُ بِعَوْنِكَ وَحَوْلِكَ وَقُوَّتِكَ وَمُسْتَعِيناً بِكَ

Allāhumma innī nawaytu tilāwata smika l-ʿaẓīmi l-aʿẓami l-kabīri l-akbari bi tilāwati l-fātiḥati (...mention the number of times..) bi niyyati ihdāʾi thawābihā ilā sayyidi l-wujūdi wa ʿala-

19 As in reciting the following in one breath without pausing: *bismillāhir-raḥmānir-raḥīmil-ḥamdu lillāhi rabbil-ʿālamīn*

20 Here, one mentions the number of times one intends to repeat the *dhikr*.

mi sh-shuhūdi sayyidinā Muḥammadin ṣalla Llāhu ʿalayhi wa sallama wa niyābatan ʿan shaykhinā wa wasīlatinā ilā Rabbinā Sīdī Abi l-ʿAbbāsi Aḥmada bni Muḥammadini t-Tijānī, raḍiya Llāhu ʿanhu. Wa aqūlu bi ʿawnika wa ḥawlika wa quwwatika wa mustaʿīnan bika.[21]

Then, one should recite *al-Fātiḥah* the specified number of times with the intention of worship. One should not make a *duʿāʾ* afterwards because *al-Fātiḥah* is the most perfect and noble of prayers.

The greatest Name which is found in *al-Fātiḥah* is obtained by selecting the non-repeating letters of the phrase *Bismillāhi r-Raḥmāni r-Raḥīmi l-Ḥamdu li-Llāh* which will yield 11 letters. These are the letters of the greatest Name. They can be arranged in different ways, the highest and greatest of which is their arrangement in *al-Fātiḥah*. The *Basmalah* of *al-Fātiḥah* is the one that contains the Power of Disposition (التَّصْرِيف), not any of the other *basmalahs* in the Quran.

Sidi Muḥy al-Dīn ibn ʿArabī said, "I worked as a servant of Sayyidah Fāṭimah, the daughter al-Muthannā, and I found her reciting al-Fātiḥah such that whenever she recited a verse a part of a human body appeared. When she finished, there was a woman standing before her. She would tell her, "Go, O *Fātiḥah*, and do such-and-such." Sayyidah Faṭimah used to say that whoever had *al-Fātiḥah* had no need of anything else.

However, reciting it with the intention of worship is supe-

21 O Allah, I intend to recite Your great and most magnificent Name, your great and most splendid Name, by reciting *al-Fātiḥah* (and then specific the number of times) with the intention of gifting the reward to the master of existence and the standard-bearer of witnessing, our master Muhammad, may Allah send His *ṣalāt* and *salām* upon him, on behalf of our Shaykh, our means to our Lord, Sidi Abu al-ʿAbbās Ahmad ibn Muhammad al-Tijani, may Allah be pleased with him. So I say with Your help, Your strength, Your power, and while seeking Your assistance.

rior to any kind of power of disposition.

صَلَاةُ الفَاتِحِ بِنِيَّةِ الإِسْمِ

Ṣalāt al-Fātiḥ with the intention of the Name

The conditions for this *dhikr* are the following:

1. Valid permission.

2. Maintaining a specific number of repetitions from among the following options: 313 or 315 or 489 or 1041 or 11 or 111 or 1111. It should be recited once in the morning and once in the evening.

3. One should bring to mind the blessed form of the Prophet ﷺ when one recites.

4. One should feel the meaning of this prayer in one's heart.

5. One must be completely convinced that one cannot fathom the great worth of the Messenger of Allah ﷺ and that Allah has allowed us to pray for *ṣalawāt* upon him on His behalf, for He alone knows the magnificent worth and esteem of His Prophet ﷺ.

6. One must recite this prayer with the intention of worship, not seeking reward or fearing punishment.

7. One should recite it with a measured and clear voice.

One should recite the following *maqṣad* before the *dhikr*.

اللَّهُمَّ إِنِّي نَوَيْتُ تِلَاوَةَ اسْمِكَ العَظِيمِ الأَعْظَمِ الكَبِيرِ الأَكْبَرِ بِتَلَاوَةِ صَلَاةِ الفَاتِحِ لِمَا أُغْلِقَ - وتُحَدِّدْ العَدَدَ[22] - بِنِيَّةِ إِهْدَاءِ ثَوَابِهَا إِلَي سَيِّدِ الوُجُودِ وَعَلَمِ الشُّهُود سَيِّدِنَا مُحَمَّدٍ صَلَّي اللهُ عَلَيْهِ وَسَلَّمَ وَنِيَابَةً عَنْ شَيْخِنَا وَوَسِيلَتِنَا إِلَي رَبِّنَا سِيدي أَبِي العَبَّاسِ أَحْمَدَ بْنِ مُحَمَّدٍ التِّجَانِي رَضِيَ اللهُ عَنْهُ وَأَقُولُ بِعَوْنِكَ وَحَوْلِكَ وَقُوَّتِكَ وَمُسْتَعِيناً بِكَ

Allāhumma innī nawaytu tilāwata smika l-ʿaẓīmi l-aʿẓami l-kabīri l-akbari bi tilāwati ṣalāti l-fātiḥi limā ughliqa (... mention the number of times..) bi niyyati ihdāʾi thawābihā ilā sayyidi l-wujūdi wa ʿalami sh-shuhūdi sayyidinā Muḥammadin ṣalla Llāhu ʿalayhi wa sallama wa niyābatan ʿan shaykhinā wa wasīlatinā ilā Rabbinā Sīdī Abi l-ʿAbbāsi Aḥmada bni Muḥammadini t-Tijānī, raḍiya Llāhu ʿanhu. Wa aqūlu bi ʿawnika wa ḥawlika wa quwwatika wa mustaʿīnan bika.[23]

Then one should recite this *dhikr* the specified number of times.

22 Here, one mentions the number of times one intends to repeat the *dhikr*.

23 O Allah, I intend to recite Your great and most magnificent Name, your great and most splendid Name, by reciting *Ṣalāt al-Fātiḥi limā ughliqa* (and then specific the number of times) with the intention of gifting the reward to the master of existence and the standard-bearer of witnessing, our master Muhammad, may Allah send His *ṣalāt* and *salām* upon him, on behalf of our Shaykh, our means to our Lord, Sidi Abu al-ʿAbbās Ahmad ibn Muhammad al-Tijani, may Allah be pleased with him. So I say with Your help, Your strength, Your power, and while seeking Your assistance.

صَلَاةُ الفَاتِحِ بِنِيَّةِ بَاطِنِ البَاطِنِ

Ṣalāt al-Fātiḥ with the intention of the inward of the inward

This *dhikr* is recited on Mondays and Fridays after the morning prayer with ritual purity derived from water or clean dirt. One may be sitting, walking, or standing and in whatever state one is in. If one recites the *wird* earlier in the night before dawn, then one should not recite this prayer at that time but wait until after the moring prayer.

It consists of reciting *Ṣālāt al-Fātiḥ* ten times. Before beginning, one says:

اللَّهُمَّ إِنِّي نَوَيْتُ أَنْ أَتَقَرَّبَ إِلَيْكَ بِتَلَاوَةِ صَلَاةِ الفَاتِحِ لِمَا أُغْلِقَ عَشَرَ مَرَّاتٍ بِمَرْتَبَةِ الظَّاهِرِ وَالبَاطِنِ وَبَاطِنِ البَاطِنِ بِنِيَّةِ إِهْدَاءِ ثَوَابِهَا إِلَى سَيِّدِ الوُجُودِ وَعَلَمِ الشُّهُودِ سَيِّدِنَا مُحَمَّدٍ صَلَّى اللهُ عَلَيْهِ وَسَلَّمَ وَنِيَابَةً عَنْ شَيْخِنَا وَوَسِيلَتِنَا إِلَى رَبِّنَا سِيدِي أَبِي العَبَّاسِ أَحْمَدَ بْنِ مُحَمَّدٍ التِّجَانِي رَضِيَ اللهُ عَنْهُ وَأَقُولُ بِعَوْنِكَ وَحَوْلِكَ وَقُوَّتِكَ وَمُسْتَعِيناً بِكَ

Allāhumma innī nawaytu an ataqarraba ilayka bi tilāwati ṣalāti l-fātiḥi limā ughliqa ʿashara marrātin bi martabati ẓ-ẓāhi-ri wa l-bāṭini wa bāṭini l-bāṭini bi niyyati ihdāʾi thawābihā ilā sayyidi l-wujūdi wa ʿalami sh-shuhūdi sayyidinā Muḥammadin ṣalla Llāhu ʿalayhi wa sallama wa niyābatan ʿan shaykhinā wa wasīlatinā ilā Rabbinā Sīdī Abi l-ʿAbbāsi Aḥmada bni Muḥam-madini t-Tijānī, raḍiya Llāhu ʿanhu. Wa aqūlu bi ʿawnika wa ḥawlika wa quwwatika wa mustaʿīnan bika.[24]

---

24 O Allah, I intend to draw near to You by reciting *Ṣalāt al-Fātiḥi limā ughliqa* ten times according the outward level, the hidden level, and the hidden of the hidden level with the intention of gifting the reward to the master of existence and the standard-bearer of witnessing, our master

سِرُّ الزِّيَارَة

The Secret of Visiting

This *dhikr* is recited after the daily *wird* in the morning and evening while one has ritually purity using water or dirt, sitting, walking, or standing and in any condition. If one recites the *wird* early, then one may also recite this early. It consists of the following words:

السَّلَامُ عَلَيْكَ أَيُّهَا النَّبِيُّ وَرَحْمَةُ اللهِ وَبَرَكَاتُهُ ١٠٠ مَرَّةٍ

السَّلَامُ عَلَيْكَ يَا سَيِّدَنَا وَمَوْلَانَا أَبَا بَكْرٍ الصِّدِّيقِ وَرَحْمَةُ اللهِ وَبَرَكَاتُهُ

السَّلَامُ عَلَيْكَ يَا سَيِّدَنَا وَمَوْلَانَا عُمَرَ بْنَ الخَطَّابِ وَرَحْمَةُ اللهِ وَبَرَكَاتُهُ

السَّلَامُ عَلَيْكَ يَا سَيِّدَنَا وَمَوْلَانَا عُثْمَانَ بْنَ عَفَّانٍ وَرَحْمَةُ اللهِ وَبَرَكَاتُهُ

السَّلَامُ عَلَيْكَ يَا سَيِّدَنَا وَمَوْلَانَا عَلِيًّا بْنَ أَبِي طَالِبٍ وَرَحْمَةُ اللهِ وَبَرَكَاتُهُ

السَّلَامُ عَلَيْكُمْ يَا أَصْحَابَ رَسُولِ اللهِ وَرَحْمَةُ اللهِ وَبَرَكَاتُهُ

السَّلَامُ عَلَيْكُمْ يَا أَهْلَ بَيْتِ رَسُولِ اللهِ الطَّاهِرِينَ المُطَهَّرِينَ وَرَحْمَةُ اللهِ وَبَرَكَاتُهُ

السَّلَامُ عَلَيْكَ يَا سَيِّدَنَا وَمَوْلَانَا أَحْمَدَ بْنَ مُحَمَّدٍ التِّجَانِيَّ وَرَحْمَةُ اللهِ وَبَرَكَاتُهُ

السَّلَامُ عَلَيْكُمْ يَا كَافَّةَ أَصْحَابِ الشَّيْخِ وَرَحْمَةُ اللهِ تَعَالَي وَبَرَكَاتُهُ

جَزَي اللهُ عَنَّا نَبِيَّنَا وَرَسُولَنَا مُحَمَّداً أَفْضَلَ مَا هُوَ أَهْلُهُ

جَزَي اللهُ عَنَّا شَيْخَنَا وَأُسْتَاذَنَا وَوَسِيلَتَنَا إِلَي رَبِّنَا القُطْبَ المَكْتُومَ وَالخَاتِمَ المُحَمَّدِيَّ المَعْلُومَ مَوْلَانَا أَحْمَدَ بْنَ مُحَمَّدٍ التِّجَانِيَّ مَا هُوَ أَهْلُهُ

Muhammad, may Allah send His *ṣalāt* and *salām* upon him, on behalf of our Shaykh, our means to our Lord, Sidi Abu al-ʿAbbās Ahmad ibn Muhammad al-Tijani, may Allah be pleased with him. So I say with Your help, Your strength, Your power, and while seeking Your assistance.

As-salāmu ʿalayka ayyuha n-nabiyyu wa raḥmatu Llāhi wa barakātuhu (100 times). As-salāmu ʿalayka yā sayyidanā wa mawlānā abā bakrini ṣ-ṣiddīqa wa raḥmatu Llāhi wa barakātuhu. As-salāmu ʿalayka yā sayyidanā wa mawlānā ʿumara bna l-khaṭṭāb wa raḥmatu Llāhi wa barakātuhu. As-salāmu ʿalayka yā sayyidanā wa mawlānā ʿuthmāna bna ʿaffānin wa raḥmatu Llāhi wa barakātuhu. As-salāmu ʿalayka yā sayyidanā wa mawlānā ʿaliyyani bna abī ṭālibin wa raḥmatu Llāhi wa barakātuhu. As-salāmu ʿalayka yā aṣḥābi rasūli Llāhi wa raḥmatu Llāhi wa barakātuhu. As-salāmu ʿalayka yā ahla bayti rasūli Llāhi aṭ-ṭāhirīna l-muṭahharīna wa raḥmatu Llāhi wa barakātuhu. As-salāmu ʿalayka yā sayyidanā wa mawlānā aḥmada bna muḥammadini t-tijānī wa raḥmatu Llāhi wa barakātuhu. As-salāmu ʿalayka yā kāffata aṣḥābi sh-shaykhi wa raḥmatu Llāhi wa barakātuhu. Jaza Llāhu ʿannā nabiyyanā wa rasūlanā sayyidanā Muḥammadan afḍala mā huwa ahluhu. Jaza Llāhu ʿannā shaykhanā wa ustādhanā wa wasīlatinā ilā rabbinā l-quṭba l-maktūma wal khātama l-muḥammadiyya l-maʿlūma mawlanā Aḥmada bna Muḥammadani t-tijānī mā huwa ahluhu.[25]

25 Peace be upon you, O Prophet, and Allah's Mercy and Blessings (100 times). Peace be upon you, O our master and protector, Abu Bakr the Believer, and Allah's Mercy and Blessings. Peace be upon you, O our master and protector, ʿUmar son of Khaṭṭāb, and Allah's Mercy and Blessings. Peace be upon you, O our master and protector, ʿUthmān son of ʿAffān, and Allah's Mercy and Blessings. Peace be upon you, O our master and protector, ʿAli son of Abu Ṭālib, and Allah's Mercy and Blessings. Peace be upon you, O companions of the Messenger of Allah, and Allah's Mercy and Blessings. Peace be upon you, O pure and purified family of the Messenger of Allah, and Allah's Mercy and Blessings. Peace be upon you, O our master and protector, Ahmad ibn Muhammad al-Tijani, and Allah's Mercy and Blessings. Peace be upon you, O companions of the Shaykh, and Allah's Mercy and Blessings. May Allah reward our prophet and messenger Muhammad on our behalf according to his greatness. May Allah reward our shakykh, teacher, and means to our Lord, the hidden pole and the verified Muhammadan seal, our protector, Ahmad the son of Muhammad al-Tijānī, on our behalf according to his greatness.

مِفْتَاحُ الْقُطْبَانِيَّة

The Key to Polehood

The name of this *dhikr* comes from the fact that whoever recites it regularly will become one of the poles, in terms of rank, not in terms of spiritual authority and power.

One recites the *Basmalah*, then *Ṣūrat al-Fātiḥah* once, and then *Ṣalāt al-Fātiḥ* 11 times. Then one recites the following words:

اللَّهُمَّ إِنِّي نَوَيْتُ أَنْ أَتَعَبَّدَ إِلَيْكَ بِتِلَاوَةِ سُورَةِ الإِخْلَاصِ أَلْف وَمائَةَ وَأَحَدَ عَشَرَ مَرَّةً تَعْظِيماً وَإِجْلَالاً لَكَ وَابْتِغَاءَ مَرْضَاتِكَ وَقَصْداً لِوَجْهِكَ الْكَرِيمِ وَالَّتِي هِيَ مِفْتَاحُ الْقُطْبَانِيَّةِ نَوَيْتُ بِتِلَاوَتِهَا اسْتِغْرَاقِ شُكْرِ مَا أَنْعَمْتَ بِهِ عَلَيَّ مِمَّا أَحَاطَ بِهِ عِلْمُكَ مِنَ النِّعَمِ الظَّاهِرَةِ وَالْبَاطِنَةِ الْمُتَقَدِّمَةِ وَالْمُتَأَخِّرَةِ مَعَ اسْتِغْرَاقِ تَعْظِيمِكَ وَتَقْدِيسِكَ وَحَمْدِكَ وَشُكْرِكَ وَتَمْجِيدِكَ حَتَّى تَكُونَ فِي كُلِّ مَرَّةٍ مِنْ تِلَاوَتِهَا عِبَادَةِ جَمِيعِ مَا أَحَاطَ بِهِ عِلْمُكَ مِنْ مَنَائِحِكَ وَفَضْلِكَ وَرِزْقِكَ وَكَرَمِكَ وَجُودِكَ وَلُطْفِكَ وَعَطَائِكَ وَرَأْفَتِكَ وَرَحْمَتِكَ وَرِضَاكَ وَعِزِّكَ وَغِنَاكَ وَمَوَاهِبِكَ الَّتِي لَا تَنْحَصِرُ وَأَنْ تُزِيلَ عَنْ رُوحِي فِي كُلِّ لَحْظَةٍ مِنْ لَحَظَاتِ فَضْلِكَ أَلْفَ أَلْفَ حِجَابٍ مِنْ حُجُبِ غُيُوبِكَ حَتَّى تُصَفِّهَا بِصَفَائِكَ الَّذِي كَانَتْ عَلَيْهِ قَبْلَ تَرْكِيبِهَا فِي الْجَسَدِ وَكُلُّ ذَلِكَ مِنْ بَابِ جُودِكَ وَكَرَمِكَ وَغِنَاكَ وَإِعْزَازِكَ لِمَنْ تَشَاءُ وَأَقُولُ بِإِمْدَادِكَ وَعَوْنِكَ وَحَوْلِكَ وَقُوَّتِكَ وَمُسْتَعِيناً بِكَ:

Allāhumma innī nawaytu an ataʿabbada ilayka bi tilāwati sūrat al-ikhlāṣi alfa wa miʾata wa aḥada ʿashara marratan taʿẓīman wa ijlālan laka wa b-tighāʾa marḍātika wa qaṣdan li wajhika l-karīmi wallatī hiya miftāḥu l-quṭbāniyyati nawaytu bi tilāwatihā stighrāqi shukri mā anʿamta bihi ʿalayya mimmā aḥāṭa bihi ʿilmuka mina n-niʿami ẓ-ẓāhirati wa l-bāṭinati l-mutaqaddimati wa l-mutaʾakhkhirati maʿa stighrāqi taʿẓīmika wa taqdīsika wa ḥamdika wa luṭfika wa shukrika wa tamjīdika ḥattā takūna fī kulli marratin min tilāwatihā ʿibādatu jamīʿi mā aḥāṭa bihi ʿilmuka min manāʾiḥika wa faḍlika wa rizqika wa karamika wa jūdika wa luṭfika wa ʿaṭāʾika wa raʾfatika wa raḥmatika wa riḍāka wa ʿizzika wa ghināka wa mawāhibika llatī lā tanḥaṣir wa an tuzīla ʿan rūḥī fī kulli laḥẓatin min laḥaẓāti faḍlika alfa alfa ḥijābin min ḥujubi ghuyūbika ḥattā tuṣaffihā bi ṣafāʾika llaẓī kānat ʿalayhi qabla tarkībihā fī l-jasadi wa kullu dhālika min bābi jūdika wa karamika wa ghināka wa iʿzāzika liman tashāʾ. Wa aqūlu bi imdādika wa ʿawnika wa ḥawlika wa quwwatika wa mustaʿīnan bika:[26]

Then one recites *Sūrat al-Ikhlāṣ* 1111 times.

After completing the recitation, one recites the following prayer:

اللّٰهُمَّ يا رَبِّ بِالْمَكْنُونِ مِنْ أَسْمائِكَ وَمَا وَارَتْهُ الْحُجُبُ مِنْ بَهائِكَ وَبِرِدَاءِ كِبْرِيَائِكَ وَإِزَارِ عَظَمَتِكَ وَسُرَادِقِ هَيْبَتِكَ وَمَا وَرَاءَ ذٰلِكَ مِمَّا

26 O Allah, I intend to worship You by reciting Surah Al-Ikhlas 1,111 times in glorification and reverence of You, seeking Your pleasure and intending Your Noble Face, which is the key to Polehood. I intend with its recitation to encompass gratitude for what You have bestowed upon me, of which Your knowledge has encompassed, of apparent and hidden blessings, both those that have preceded and those that will come, along with encompassing Your glorification, sanctification, praise, gratitude, and exaltation, so that with each recitation, it becomes an act of worship for all that Your knowledge has encompassed of Your favors, blessings, sustenance, generosity, bounty, kindness, gifts, compassion, mercy, pleasure, honor, self-sufficiency, and inexhaustible gifts. I ask that You remove from my soul, with each moment of Your grace, a million veils from the veils of Your mysteries, until You purify it with Your purity that it had before being composed in the body. All of this is from the door of Your generosity, honor, self-sufficiency, and empowering whomsoever You will, and I say with Your support, assistance, power, strength, and seeking help from You..

لَا يَحِيطُ بِهِ إِلَّا أَنْتَ اجْعَلْنِي مَصُوناً بِصَوْنِكَ مُحَاطاً بِعَوْنِكَ مَسْتُوراً بِنُورِكَ ظَاهِراً بِظُهُورِكَ غَنِيّاً بِعَطَائِكَ مَأْنُوساً بِأَلْطَافِكَ مَحْرُوساً بِإِسْعَافِكَ مَقْبُولاً بِفَضْلِكَ مَكْفُولاً بِعَطَائِكَ. أَسْأَلُكَ بِكُلِّ مَا وَجَبَ لِذَاتِكَ مِنْ أَسْمَائِكَ وَصِفَاتِكَ وَبِكُلِّ مَا دَعَاكَ بِهِ الدَّاعُونَ وَقَصَدَكَ بِهِ الْقَاصِدُونَ وَذَكَرَكَ بِهِ الذَّاكِرُونَ وَسَبَّحَكَ بِهِ الْمُسَبِّحُونَ وَقَدَّسَكَ بِهِ الْمُقَدِّسُونَ وَحَمَدَكَ بِهِ الْحَامِدُونَ وَبِكُلِّ مَا أَثْنَيْتَ بِهِ عَلَىٰ نَفْسِكَ فِي نَفْسِكَ وَبِكُلِّ مَا أَجْرَيْتَهُ عَلَىٰ أَلْسِنَةِ خَلْقِكَ فِي جَمِيعِ كَوْنِكَ اجْعَلْنِي بِعِنَايَتِكَ مَشْمُولاً بِنُورِكَ مَوْصُولاً فِي يَقَظَاتِي وَغَفَلَاتِي وَحَرَكَاتِي وَسَكَنَاتِي وَفِي حَيَاتِي وَمَمَاتِي وَفِي كُلِّ جِهَاتِي وَبِنُورِ وَجْهِكَ السَّاطِعِ وَحُكْمِكَ الْقَاطِعِ وَقَهْرِكَ الْقَامِعِ اجْعَلْ لِي مِنْ نَفْسِكَ عِنْدَ نَفْسِكَ شَافِعاً وَادْفَعْ عَنِّي جَمِيعَ الْمَضَارِّ وَاجْلِبْ لِي جَمِيعَ الْمَنَافِعِ بِنَصِّ حَكِيمٍ لَهُ سِرٌّ قَاطِعٌ

Allahumma ya rabbi bil-maknooni min asmaa'ika wa maa waarathul-hujubu min bahaa'ika wa biridaa'i kibriyaa'ika wa izaari 'azamatika wa suradiqi haibatika wa maa waraa'a dhaalika mimmaa laa yahitubihi illa anta, ij'alni masoonan bi-saunik, muhaatan bi-'awnika, mustooran binuurika, dhaahira bi-zhuhoorika, ghaniyyan bi-'ataa'ika, ma'noosan bi-altaafika, mahruusan bi-is'aafika, maqboolan bifadlik, makfuulan bi-'ataa'ika. As'aluka bikulli maa wajaba lidhaatika min asmaa'ika wa sifaatika wa bikulli maa da'aaka bihi d-daa'uuna wa qasadaka bihi-l-qaasiduuna wa dhakaraka bihi-dh-dhaakiruuna wa sabbahaka bihi-l-musabbihuuna wa qaddasaka bihi-l-muqaddisuuna wa hamadaka bihi-l-haamiduuna wa bikulli maa athnayta bihi 'alaa nafsika fi nafsika, wa bikulli maa ajraytahu 'alayya al-sinat khalqika fi jami'i kawnika, ij'alni bi-'inaayatika mashmuulan binuurika mawsulan fi yaqzaati wa ghafalaati wa harakati wa sakanaati wa fi hayati wa mamaati wa fi kulli jihati wa binuuri wajhika as-saati'i wa hukmika-l-qaati'i wa qahril-qam'i'i, ij'al li min nafsika 'inda nafsika shafi'an wa adfa' 'anni jami'a-l-madaarri wa ajlib li jami'a-l-manaafi'i binassin hakeemin lahu sirrun qaati'un.[27]

دَائِرَةُ الإِحَاطَة
The Circle of Encompassment

Many spiritual masters of Islam have various "Circles of Encompassment," but their chains of transmission are often disconnected. The following Circle of Encompassment has an authentic chain of transmission going back to Shaykh al-Tijānī ﷺ.

One recites the *following*:

1. *Ṣūrat al-Fātiḥah* once.

2. *Ṣalāt al-Fātiḥ* once.

3. Then one recites:

---

27 O Allah, O Lord, by the concealed of Your Names and what the veils hide of Your splendor, by the mantle of Your pride and the garment of Your greatness, by the curtain of Your awe and what is beyond that which none can encompass except You, make me protected by Your preservation, surrounded by Your aid, concealed by Your light, manifested by Your manifestation, enriched by Your bounty, familiar with Your subtleties, guarded by Your protection, accepted by Your grace, and fulfilled by Your gifts. I ask You by all that is required of Your Essence through Your Names and Attributes, by all that the callers have called upon You, by all that the seekers have sought from You, by all that the rememberers have mentioned You, by all that the praisers have praised You, by all that the sanctifiers have sanctified You, by all that You have praised Yourself with within Yourself, and by all that You have made flow on the tongues of Your creation in all of Your universe, make me, by Your care, encompassed by Your light, connected to You in my wakefulness and my heedlessness, in my movements and my stillness, in my life and my death, and in every direction. By the light of Your shining Face, Your decisive judgment, and Your overpowering dominion, make an intercessor for me from Yourself, near You, repel from me all harm, and bring to me all benefits with a wise decree that has a decisive secret.

سُبْحَانَ رَبِّكَ رَبِّ الْعِزَّةِ عَمَّا يَصِفُونَ ۝ وَسَلَامٌ عَلَى الْمُرْسَلِينَ ۝
وَالْحَمْدُ لِلَّهِ رَبِّ الْعَالَمِينَ ۝

subḥāna rabbika rabbil-ʿizzati ʿammā yaṣifūn, wa salāmun ʿalal-mursalīn, wal-ḥamdu lillāhi rabbil-ʿālamīn.

4. Then one recites the following prayer:

اللَّهُمَّ إِنِّي نَوَيْتُ أَنْ أَتَقَرَّبَ إِلَيْكَ بِتِلَاوَةِ أَسْمَائِكَ الْعِظَامِ الْبَاطِنَةِ وَالَّتِي هِيَ سِرُّ الْقُرْآنِ وَنُورُ الْفُرْقَانِ وَبَاطِنِ التَّنْزِيلِ وَرُوحِ التَّأْوِيلِ اللَّهُمَّ نَوَيْتُ بِذِكْرِهَا التَّمْجِيدَ وَالتَّحْمِيدِ وَالتَّقْدِيسَ لِذَاتِكَ الْعَلِيَّةِ اِمْتِثَالًا لَكَ وَخُضُوعًا لِأَمْرِكَ بِمَا فِي ذَلِكَ الإِحَاطَةِ بِجَمِيعِ أَذْكَارِ الذَّاكِرِينَ، وَتِلَاوَةِ التَّالِينَ مِنْ لَدُنْ سَيِّدِنَا آدَمَ إِلَى يَوْمِ الدِّينِ، بِنِيَّةِ إِهْدَاءِ ثَوَابِهَا إِلَى سَيِّدِ الْوُجُودِ وَعَلَمِ الشُّهُودِ سَيِّدِنَا مُحَمَّدٍ وَنِيَابَةً عَنْ شَيْخِنَا وَوَسِيلَتِنَا إِلَى رَبِّنَا سَيِّدِي أَحْمَدَ بِنِ مُحَمَّدٍ التَّجَانِيِّ وَأَقُولُ بِعَوْنِكَ وَحولِكَ وَقُوَّتِكَ وَمُسْتَعِينًا بِكَ

بِسْمِ اللهِ الرَّحْمَنِ الرَّحِيمِ

۝ الم - المص - الر - المر - كهيعص - حم عسق - حم - طس -
طسم - طه - يس - ص - ق - ن ۝

صَدَقَ اللهُ الْعَظِيم

Allāhumma innī nawaytu an ataqarraba ilayka bitilāwati asma'ika al-'aẓhāmi al-bāṭinah, wa-llatī hiya sirru al-Qur'āni wa-nūru al-furqāni, wa-bāṭini al-tanzīli wa-rūḥi al-ta'wīli. Allāhumma nawaytu bidhikrihā al-tamjīda wa-al-taḥmīda wa-al-taqdīsa li dhātika al-'aliyyah, imtithālan laka wa-khuḍū'an li-amrik, bimā fī dhālika al-iḥāṭah bi-jamī'i aẓkāri al-dhākirīna, wa-tilāwati al-tālīna min ladun sayyidinā Ādama ilā yawmi al-dīn, binīyatihā ihdā'i thawābihā ilā sayyidi al-wujūdi wa-'alam al-shuhūdi sayyidinā Muḥammadin wa-niyābatan 'an shaykhinā wa-wasīlatinā ilā rabbinā sayyidī Aḥmada bin Muḥammadin al-Tajānī. Wa-aqūlu bi-'awnika wa-ḥūlika wa-quwwatika wa-musta'īnan bika.

Bismi Llāhi r-raḥmāni r-raḥīmi.

Alif Lām Mīm - Alif Lām Mīm Ṣād - Alif Lām Rā - Alif Lām Mīm Rā - Kāf Hā Yā 'Ayn Ṣād - Hā Mīm 'Ayn Sīn Qāf - Ḥā Mīm - Ṭā Sīn - Ṭā Sīn Mīm - Ṭā Hā - Yā Sīn - Ṣād - Qāf - Nūn

Ṣadaqa Allāhu al-'Āẓīm[28]

You may recite these great names throughout the day for any number of times that you decidee for oneself, and it is also permissible to recite it once only.

Finally, one concludes with this prayer:

يا مَنْ أَظْهَرَ الجْمِيلَ وَسَتَرَ القَبِيحَ ولَمْ يُؤاخِذْ بِالجَرِيرَةِ وَلَمْ يَهْتِكِ

28 O Allah, I intend to draw closer to You by reciting Your Names, including the Innermost Essence which is the secret of the Quran, the light of the Furqan, the essence of the Revelation, and the soul of interpretation. O Allah, I intend to extol and glorify Your lofty essence and to comply with Your commandments, thereby encompassing all the remembrances of the those who mention You and all the recitations of the reciters, from the time of our master Adam until the Day of Judgment, with the intention of dedicating its rewards to the Lord of existence, the knowledge of the witnesses, our master Muhammad, and on behalf of our shaykh and as a means to approach our Lord, our master Ahmad bin Muhammad Al-Tijani. And I say this with Your help, support, power, and by seeking Your aid.

In the name of Allah, the Most Merciful, the Compassionate.

Alif Lām Mīm - Alif Lām Mīm Ṣād - Alif Lām Rā - Alif Lām Mīm Rā - Kāf Hā Yā 'Ayn Ṣād - Hā Mīm 'Ayn Sīn Qāf - Ḥā Mīm - Ṭā Sīn - Ṭā Sīn Mīm - Ṭā Hā - Yā Sīn - Ṣād - Qāf - Nūn

Allah the Almighty has spoken the truth.

السِّتْرَ ويا عَظِيمَ الْعفوِ ويا حَسَنَ التَّجاوُزِ ويا وَاسِعَ الْمَغْفِرَةِ ويا باسِطَ الْيَدَينِ بِالرَّحْمَةِ ويا سامِعَ كُلِّ نَجْوَى وَيا مُنْتَهَى كُلِّ شَكْوَى ويا كَرِيمَ الصَّفحِ ويا عَظِيمَ الْمَنِّ وَيَا مُقِيلَ الْعَثَرَاتِ ويا مُبْتَدِئاً بِالنِّعَمِ قَبْلَ اسْتِحْقاقِها يا رَبِّي وَيا سَيِّدي وَيا مَوْلاَيَ وَيا غايَةَ رَغْبَتِي أَسْأَلُكَ أَلاَّ تُشَوِّهَ خِلْقَتِي بِبَلاءِ الدُنْيا ولا بِعَذابِ النَّارِ

Yā man aẓ-hara l-jamīl / wa satara l-qabīḥ / wa lam yu'ākh-idh bi l-jarīrah / wa lam yah-tiki s-sitr / wa yā 'aẓīma l-'afw / wa yā ḥasana t-tajā-wuz / wa yā wāsi'a l-magh-fira / wa yā bāṣiṭa l-yaday-ni bi r-raḥma / wa yā sāmi'a kulli najwā / wa yā muntahā kulli shakwā / wa yā karīma ṣ-ṣaf-ḥ / wa yā 'aẓī-ma l-mann / wa yā muqīla l-'atharāt / wa yā mub-ta-di'an bi n-ni'ami qabla s-tiḥ-qā-qihā / yā rabbī / wa yā sayyidī / wa yā mawlāy / wa yā ghā-yata ragh-batī / as'aluka al-lā tu-shaw wih-ha khilqatī bi balā'i d-dunyā wa lā bi 'a-dhā-bi n-nār

أَللّٰهُمَّ إِنِّي أَعُوذُ بِرِضَاكَ مِنْ سَخَطِكَ وَبِمُعَافَاتِكَ مِنْ عُقُوبَتِكَ وَأَعُوذُ بِكَ مِنْكَ لَا أُحْصِي ثَنَاءً عَلَيْكَ أَنْتَ كَمَا أَثْنَيْتَ عَلَى نَفْسِكَ أَللّٰهُمَّ إِنِّي أَسْأَلُكَ حُبَّكَ وَرِضَاكَ وَالنَّظَرَ إِلَي وَجْهِكَ الْكَرِيمِ

Allahumma inni a'oodhu biridaaka min sakhatika wa bimu'aafaatika min 'uqubatika wa a'oodhu bika minka laa uhsi thanaa'an 'alayka anta kamaa athnayta 'alaa nafsik. Allahumma inni as'aluka hubbaka wa ridaka wal-nazara ila wajhika al-kareem.[29]

Some rules regarding this prayer:

1. One must be in a state of wudū and one's clothes and place of prayer must be ritually pure.

---

29 O Allah, I seek refuge in Your pleasure from Your wrath, and in Your pardon from Your punishment, and I seek refuge in You from You. I cannot enumerate the praises due to You; You are as You have praised Yourself. O Allah, I ask You for Your love, Your pleasure, and the vision of Your Noble Face.

2. One may recite this prayer walking or riding.

3. One should extend the recitation of the letters contained in this phrase نَقَص عَسَلُكُمْ for the length of six short vowels (*ḥarakāt*). This is called the long elongation.

4. One should extend the recitation of the letters contained in this phrase حَيٌّ طَاهِرْ for the length of two short vowels (*ḥarakāt*). This is called the natural elongation.

5. The other letters should not be elongated.

دَائِرَةُ إِحَاطَةِ الإِسْمِ الأَعْظَمِ الكَبِير

The Circle of Encompassment of the Greatest and Most Expansive Name

One recites the *following*:

1. *Ṣūrat al-Fātiḥah* once.

2. *Ṣalāt al-Fātiḥ* once.

3. Then one recites:

سُبْحَانَ رَبِّكَ رَبِّ الْعِزَّةِ عَمَّا يَصِفُونَ ۝ وَسَلَامٌ عَلَى الْمُرْسَلِينَ ۝
وَالْحَمْدُ للهِ رَبِّ الْعَالَمِينَ ۝

subḥāna rabbika rabbil-ʿizzati ʿammā yaṣifūn, wa salāmun ʿalal-mursalīn, wal-ḥamdu lillāhi rabbil-ʿālamīn.

4. Then one recites the following prayer:

اللهُمَّ إِنِّي نَوَيْتُ تِلَاوَةَ اسْمِكَ العَظِيمِ الأَعْظَمِ الكَبِيرِ الأَكْبَرِ - وَتُحَدِّدْ

العَدَد - بِنِيَّةِ إِهْدَاءِ ثَوَابِهَا إِلَي سَيِّدِ الوُجُودِ وَعَلَمِ الشُّهُود سَيِّدِنَا مُحَمَّدٍ صَلَّى اللهُ عَلَيْهِ وَسَلَّمَ وَنِيَابَةً عَنْ شَيْخِنَا وَوَسِيلَتِنَا إِلَي رَبِّنَا سِيدي أَبِي العَبَّاسِ أَحْمَدَ بْنِ مُحَمَّدٍ التِّجَانِي رَضِيَ اللهُ عَنْهُ وَأَقُولُ بِعَوْنِكَ وَحَوْلِكَ وَقُوَّتِكَ وَمُسْتَعِيناً بِكَ

Allāhumma innī nawaytu an ataqarraba ilayka bi tilāwati ismika al-ʿaẓīmi l-aʿẓami l-kabīri l-akbar - mention the number of times here - *bi niyyati ihdāʾi thawābihā ilā sayyidi l-wujūdi wa ʿalami sh-shuhūdi sayyidinā Muḥammadin ṣalla Llāhu ʿalayhi wa sallama wa niyābatan ʿan shaykhinā wa wasīlatinā ilā Rabbinā Sīdī Abi l-ʿAbbāsi Aḥmada bni Muḥammadini t-Tijānī, raḍiya Llāhu ʿanhu. Wa aqūlu bi ʿawnika wa ḥawlika wa quwwatika wa mustaʿīnan bika.*[30]

Then one recites the specified number of times.

Rules for this prayer:

1. The allowed numbers are 100, 200, 300, 400, 500, 600, 700, 800, 900, or 1000 times.

2. After each hundred, one should make a prayer from the Quran; one may also say a single prayer at the completion of the remembrance.

3. One can recite this prayer walking or riding as long as one's place and shoes are ritually clean.

4. Ritually purity must be obtained by water.

5. One cannot interrupt the remembrance unless out of

30 O Allah, I intend to draw near to You by reciting *Ṣalāt al-Fātiḥi limā ughliqa* ten times according the outward level, the hidden level, and the hidden of the hidden level with the intention of gifting the reward to the master of existence and the standard-bearer of witnessing, our master Muhammad, may Allah send His *ṣalāt* and *salām* upon him, on behalf of our Shaykh, our means to our Lord, Sidi Abu al-ʿAbbās Ahmad ibn Muhammad al-Tijani, may Allah be pleased with him. So I say with Your help, Your strength, Your power, and while seeking Your assistance.

necessity.

6. The greatest and most expansive Name is never written, rather it is recieved directly through spiritual transmission from the essence of the Shaykh ﷺ.

Chapter 9

PRAYERS FROM THE QURAN

﴿ٱهْدِنَا ٱالصِّرَٰطَ ٱالْمُسْتَقِيمَ صِرَٰطَ ٱالَّذِينَ أَنْعَمْتَ عَلَيْهِمْ غَيْرِ ٱالْمَغْضُوبِ عَلَيْهِمْ وَلَا ٱالضَّآلِّينَ﴾

[الفاتحة: ٦-٧]

Ihdina ṣ-ṣirāṭa l-mustaqīma ۝ ṣirāṭa l-ladhīna anʿamta ʿalay-him ۝ ghayri l-maghḍūbi ʿalayhim wala ḍ-ḍāllīn[31]

﴿رَبَّنَا تَقَبَّلْ مِنَّآ إِنَّكَ أَنتَ ٱالسَّمِيعُ ٱالْعَلِيمُ﴾

[البقرة: ٧٢١]

Rabbanā taqabbal minnā innaka anta s-samīʿu l-ʿalīm[32]

﴿رَبَّنَآ ءَاتِنَا فِى ٱالدُّنْيَا حَسَنَةً وَفِى الْآخِرَةِ حَسَنَةً وَقِنَا عَذَابَ ٱالنَّارِ﴾

[البقرة: ١٠٢]

---

31 Guide us to the straight path. The path of those whom You have favored, not of those who have earned anger or of those who have gone astray. [Quran 1:6-7] And the concluding word, "Amen," is a supplication that means "O Allah, accept (this prayer)."

32 Our Lord, accept [this] from us. Indeed You are the Hearing, the Knowing. [Quran 2:127]

Rabbanā ātinā fī ad-dunyā ḥasanatan wa-fīl-ākhirati ḥasanatan wa-qinā ʿadhāba-n-nār[33]

﴿رَبَّنَآ أَفۡرِغۡ عَلَيۡنَا صَبۡرٗا وَثَبِّتۡ أَقۡدَامَنَا وَٱنصُرۡنَا عَلَى ٱلۡقَوۡمِ ٱلۡكَٰفِرِينَ﴾

[البقرة: ٢٥٠]

Rabbanā afrigh ʿalaynā ṣabrān, wa-thabbit aqdāmanā, wa-nsurnā ʿalāl-qawmi-l-kāfirīn.[34]

﴿رَبَّنَا لَا تُؤَاخِذْنَا إِنْ نَسِينَا أَوْ أَخْطَأْنَا ۚ رَبَّنَا وَلَا تَحْمِلْ عَلَيْنَا إِصْرًا كَمَا حَمَلْتَهُ عَلَى الَّذِينَ مِنْ قَبْلِنَا ۚ رَبَّنَا وَلَا تُحَمِّلْنَا مَا لَا طَاقَةَ لَنَا بِهِ ۖ وَاعْفُ عَنَّا وَاغْفِرْ لَنَا وَارْحَمْنَا ۚ أَنْتَ مَوْلَانَا فَانْصُرْنَا عَلَى الْقَوْمِ الْكَافِرِينَ﴾

[البقرة: ٢٨٦]

Rabbanā lā tuʾākhidh-nā in-nasīnā aw akhṭaʾ-nā, Rabbanā wa-lā taḥmil ʿalaynā iṣran kamā ḥamaltahu ʿalāl-ladhīna min qablina, Rabbanā wa-lā tuḥammilnā mā lā ṭāqata lanā bihi, waʿfu ʿannā, waghfir lanā, warḥamnā, anta mawlānā fansurnā ʿalal-qawmi-l-kāfirīn.[35]

---

33 Our Lord, give us good in this world and good in the Hereafter and protect us from the punishment of the Fire. [Quran 2:201]

34 Our Lord, pour upon us patience and plant firmly our feet and give us victory over the disbelieving people. [Quran 2:250]

35 Our Lord, do not impose blame upon us if we have forgotten or erred. Our Lord, and lay not upon us a burden like that which You laid upon those before us. Our Lord, and burden us not with that which we have no ability to bear. And pardon us; and forgive us; and have mercy upon us. You are our protector, so give us victory over the disbelieving people. [Quran 2:286]

﴿رَبَّنَا لَا تُزِغْ قُلُوبَنَا بَعْدَ إِذْ هَدَيْتَنَا وَهَبْ لَنَا مِن لَّدُنكَ رَحْمَةً إِنَّكَ أَنتَ الْوَهَّابُ﴾

[آل عمران: ٨]

Rabbanā lā tuzigh qulūbanā baʿda idh hadaytanā, wa-hab lanā min ladunka raḥmatan, innaka anta-l-wahhāb.[36]

﴿رَبَّنَا إِنَّنَا آمَنَّا فَاغْفِرْ لَنَا ذُنُوبَنَا وَقِنَا عَذَابَ النَّارِ﴾

[آل عمران: ١٦]

Rabbanā innanā āmannā faghfir lanā dhunūbanā wa-qinā ʿadhāba-n-nār.[37]

﴿رَبِّ هَبْ لِي مِن لَّدُنكَ ذُرِّيَّةً طَيِّبَةً إِنَّكَ سَمِيعُ الدُّعَاءِ﴾

[آل عمران: ٣٨]

Rabbi hab lī min ladunka dhurriyyatan ṭayyibatan, innaka samīʿu-d-duʿā.[38]

﴿رَبَّنَا آمَنَّا بِمَا أَنزَلْتَ وَاتَّبَعْنَا الرَّسُولَ فَاكْتُبْنَا مَعَ الشَّاهِدِينَ﴾

[آل عمران: ٥٣]

Rabbanā āmannā bimā anzalta wattabaʿnā ar-rasūla fa-ktubnā maʿa ash-shāhidīn.[39]

﴿رَبَّنَا اغْفِرْ لَنَا ذُنُوبَنَا وَإِسْرَافَنَا فِي أَمْرِنَا وَثَبِّتْ أَقْدَامَنَا وَانصُرْنَا عَلَى

---

36 Our Lord, let not our hearts deviate after You have guided us and grant us from Yourself mercy. Indeed, You are the Bestower. [Quran 3:8]

37 Our Lord, indeed we have believed, so forgive us our sins and protect us from the punishment of the Fire. [Quran 3:16]

38 My Lord, grant me [a child] from Yourself who is pure. Indeed, You are the Hearer of supplication. [Quran 3:38]

39 Our Lord, we have believed in what You revealed and have followed the messenger, so register us among the witnesses [to truth]. [Quran 3:53]

الْقَوْمِ الْكَافِرِينَ﴾

[آل عمران: ١٤٧]

Rabbanā ghfir lanā dhunūbanā wa-isrāfanā fī amrinā wa-thabbit aqdāmanā wa-nsurnā ʿalal-qawmi-l-kāfirīn.[40]

﴿رَبَّنَا إِنَّنَا سَمِعْنَا مُنَادِيًا يُنَادِي لِلْإِيمَانِ أَنْ آمِنُوا بِرَبِّكُمْ فَآمَنَّا رَبَّنَا فَاغْفِرْ لَنَا ذُنُوبَنَا وَكَفِّرْ عَنَّا سَيِّئَاتِنَا وَتَوَفَّنَا مَعَ الْأَبْرَارِ رَبَّنَا وَآتِنَا مَا وَعَدْتَنَا عَلَىٰ رُسُلِكَ وَلَا تُخْزِنَا يَوْمَ الْقِيَامَةِ إِنَّكَ لَا تُخْلِفُ الْمِيعَادَ﴾

[آل عمران: ١٩٣-١٩٤]

Rabbanā innanā samiʿnā munādīan yunādī lil-īmāni an āminū birabbikum fa-āmannā, rabbanā faghfir lanā dhunūbanā wa-kaffir ʿannā sayyiʾātinā wa-tawaffanā maʿa-l-abrār. Rabbanā wa-ātinā mā waʿadtanā ʿalā rusulika wa-lā tukhzinā yawma-l-qiyāmah, innaka lā tukhlifu-l-mīʿād.[41]

﴿رَبَّنَا ظَلَمْنَا أَنفُسَنَا وَإِن لَّمْ تَغْفِرْ لَنَا وَتَرْحَمْنَا لَنَكُونَنَّ مِنَ الْخَاسِرِينَ﴾

[الأعراف: ٢٣]

Rabbanā thalamnā anfusanā wa-in lam taghfir lanā wa-tarḥamnā lanakunanna mina-l-khāsirīn.[42]

---

40 Our Lord, forgive us our sins and our excesses in our affairs and plant firmly our feet and give us victory over the disbelieving people. [Quran 3:147]

41 Our Lord, we have heard a caller calling to faith, [saying], "Believe in your Lord," and we have believed. Our Lord, forgive us our sins and remove from us our misdeeds and cause us to die with the righteous. Our Lord, grant us what You promised us through Your messengers and do not disgrace us on the Day of Resurrection. Indeed, You do not fail in [Your] promise. [Quran 3:193-194]

42 Our Lord, we have wronged ourselves, and if You do not forgive us and have mercy upon us, we will surely be among the losers. [Quran 7:23]

﴿رَبَّنَا افْتَحْ بَيْنَنَا وَبَيْنَ قَوْمِنَا بِالْحَقِّ وَأَنْتَ خَيْرُ الْفَاتِحِينَ﴾

[الأعراف: ٩٨]

Rabbanā iftaḥ baynanā wa-bayna qawminā bil-ḥaqqi wa-anta khayru-l-fātiḥīn.[43]

﴿رَبَّنَا أَفْرِغْ عَلَيْنَا صَبْرًا وَتَوَفَّنَا مُسْلِمِينَ﴾

[الأعراف: ٦٢١]

Rabbanā afrigh ʿalaynā ṣabrān wa tawaffanā muslimīn.[44]

﴿أَنْتَ وَلِيُّنَا فَٱغْفِرْ لَنَا وَٱرْحَمْنَاۖ وَأَنتَ خَيْرُ ٱلْغَٰفِرِينَ﴾

[الأعراف: ٥٥١]

Anta waliyyunā fa-ghfir lanā warḥamnā, wa-anta khayru-l-ghāfirīn.[45]

﴿رَبَّنَا لَا تَجْعَلْنَا فِتْنَةً لِّلْقَوْمِ ٱلظَّٰلِمِينَ ۝٨٥ وَنَجِّنَا بِرَحْمَتِكَ مِنَ ٱلْقَوْمِ ٱلْكَٰفِرِينَ﴾

[يونس: ٥٨-٦٨]

Rabbanā lā tajʿalnā fitnatan lil-qawmi-l-ẓālimīn, wa-najjinā bi-raḥmatika mina-l-qawmi-l-kāfirīn.[46]

﴿فَاطِرَ ٱلسَّمَٰوَٰتِ وَٱلْأَرْضِ أَنتَ وَلِيِّۦ فِي ٱلدُّنْيَا وَٱلْأٓخِرَةِۖ تَوَفَّنِي مُسْلِمًا وَأَلْحِقْنِي بِٱلصَّٰلِحِينَ﴾

[يوسف: ١٠١]

43 Our Lord, judge between us and our people in truth, and You are the best of those who give judgment. [Quran 7:89]

44 Our Lord, pour upon us patience and let us die as Muslims [in submission to You]. [Quran 7:126]

45 You are our Protector, so forgive us and have mercy upon us; and You are the best of forgivers. [Quran 7:155]

46 Our Lord, do not make us a trial for the wrongdoing people, and save us by Your mercy from the disbelieving people. [Quran 10:85-86]

Fāṭira-s-samāwāti wa-l-arḍi, anta waliyyī fī-d-dunyā wa-l-ākhirah, tawaffanī musliman wa-alḥiqnī bi-ṣ-ṣāliḥīn.[47]

﴿رَبِّ ٱجۡعَلۡنِي مُقِيمَ ٱلصَّلَوٰةِ وَمِن ذُرِّيَّتِيۚ رَبَّنَا وَتَقَبَّلۡ دُعَآءِ ۝٤٠ رَبَّنَا ٱغۡفِرۡ لِي وَلِوَٰلِدَيَّ وَلِلۡمُؤۡمِنِينَ يَوۡمَ يَقُومُ ٱلۡحِسَابُ﴾

[إبراهيم: ٤٠-٤١]

Rabbijʿalnī muqīmaṣ-ṣalāti wa-min dhurriyyatī, rabbana wa taqabbal duʿāʾi. Rabbana-ghfir lī wa-li-wālidayya wa-li-l-muʾminīna yawma yaqūmu-l-ḥisābu.[48]

﴿رَّبِّ أَدۡخِلۡنِي مُدۡخَلَ صِدۡقٖ وَأَخۡرِجۡنِي مُخۡرَجَ صِدۡقٖ وَٱجۡعَل لِّي مِن لَّدُنكَ سُلۡطَٰنٗا نَّصِيرٗا﴾

[الإسراء: ٨٠]

Rabbī adkhilnī mudkhala ṣidqin wa akhrijnī mukhraja ṣidqin, wajʿal lī min ladunka sulṭānan naṣīrā.[49]

﴿رَبَّنَآ ءَاتِنَا مِن لَّدُنكَ رَحۡمَةٗ وَهَيِّئۡ لَنَا مِنۡ أَمۡرِنَا رَشَدٗا﴾

[الكهف: ١٠]

Rabbana ātinā min ladunka raḥmah, wa hayyiʾ lana min amrinā rashadā.[50]

﴿رَبِّ ٱشۡرَحۡ لِي صَدۡرِي ۝٢٥ وَيَسِّرۡ لِيٓ أَمۡرِي ۝٢٦ وَٱحۡلُلۡ عُقۡدَةٗ مِّن

---

47 Creator of the heavens and the earth, You are my Protector in this world and in the Hereafter. Cause me to die as a Muslim and join me with the righteous. [Quran 12:101]

48 My Lord, make me one who establishes prayer, and from my descendants [as well]. Our Lord, accept my supplication. Our Lord, forgive me and my parents and the believers the Day the account is established. [Quran 14:40-41]

49 My Lord, admit me to a sound entrance and exit and grant me from Yourself a supporting authority. [Quran 17:80]

50 Our Lord, grant us mercy from Yourself, and facilitate for us our affair in the right way. [Quran 18:10]

﴿لِّسَانِي ٢٧ يَفۡقَهُواْ قَوۡلِي﴾

[طه: ٥٢-٨٢]

Rabbishrah li ṣadrī, wayassir lī amrī, Wahlul ʿuqdatan min lisānī, yafqahu qawlī.[51]

﴿رَّبِّ زِدۡنِي عِلۡمٗا﴾

[طه: ٤١١]

Rabbi zidnī ʿilmā.[52]

﴿أَنِّي مَسَّنِيَ ٱلضُّرُّ وَأَنتَ أَرۡحَمُ ٱلرَّٰحِمِينَ﴾

[الأنبياء: ٣٨]

Annī massaniyaḍ-ḍurru wa-anta arḥamu-rrāḥimīn.[53]

﴿لَّآ إِلَٰهَ إِلَّآ أَنتَ سُبۡحَٰنَكَ إِنِّي كُنتُ مِنَ ٱلظَّٰلِمِينَ﴾

[الأنبياء: ٧٨]

Lā ilāha illā anta subḥānaka innī kuntu minaẓ-ẓālimīn.[54]

﴿رَبِّ لَا تَذَرۡنِي فَرۡدٗا وَأَنتَ خَيۡرُ ٱلۡوَٰرِثِينَ﴾

[الأنبياء: ٩٨]

Rabbī lā tadharnī fardan wa-anta khayru al-wārithīn.[55]

---

51 My Lord, expand for me my chest [with assurance], and ease for me my task, and untie the knot from my tongue, that they may understand my speech. [Quran 20:25-28]

52 My Lord, increase me in knowledge. [Quran 20:114]

53 "Verily, adversity has touched me, and You are the Most Merciful of all those who show mercy." [Quran 21:83]

54 There is no deity except You; exalted are You. Indeed, I have been of the wrongdoers. [Quran 21:87]

55 My Lord, do not leave me alone [with no heir], while you are the best of inheritors. [Quran 21:89]

﴿رَّبِّ أَعُوذُ بِكَ مِنْ هَمَزَٰتِ ٱلشَّيَـٰطِينِ ﴿٩٧﴾ وَأَعُوذُ بِكَ رَبِّ أَن يَحْضُرُونِ﴾

[المؤمنون: ٨٩-٧٩]

Rabbi a'ūdhu bika min hamazāti ash-shayātīni wa a'ūdhu bika Rabbī an yaḥḍurūn.[56]

﴿رَّبِّ ٱغْفِرْ وَٱرْحَمْ وَأَنتَ خَيْرُ ٱلرَّٰحِمِينَ﴾

[المؤمنون: ٨١١]

Rabbighfir warḥam wa-anta khayru r-raḥimīn.[57]

﴿رَبَّنَا ٱصْرِفْ عَنَّا عَذَابَ جَهَنَّمَ ۖ إِنَّ عَذَابَهَا كَانَ غَرَامًا﴾

[الفرقان: ٥٦]

Rabbana isrif 'annā 'adhāba jahannama, inna 'adhābahā kāna gharaman.[58]

﴿رَبَّنَا هَبْ لَنَا مِنْ أَزْوَٰجِنَا وَذُرِّيَّـٰتِنَا قُرَّةَ أَعْيُنٍ وَٱجْعَلْنَا لِلْمُتَّقِينَ إِمَامًا﴾

[الفرقان: ٤٧]

Rabbanā hab lana min azwājinā wa dhurriyyātinā qurrata a'yunin wa ij'alnā lil-muttaqīna imāmā.[59]

﴿رَبِّ هَبْ لِى حُكْمًا وَأَلْحِقْنِى بِٱلصَّـٰلِحِينَ ﴿٨٣﴾ وَٱجْعَل لِّى لِسَانَ صِدْقٍ

---

56 My Lord, I seek refuge in You from the incitements of the devils, and I seek refuge in You, my Lord, lest they be present with me. [Quran 23:97-98]

57 My Lord, forgive and have mercy, for You are the Best of those who show mercy. [Quran 23:118]

58 Our Lord, avert from us the punishment of Hell. Indeed, its punishment is ever adhering. [Quran 25:65]

59 Our Lord, grant us from among our wives and offspring comfort to our eyes and make us an example for the righteous. [Quran 25:74]

﴿فِي ٱلۡأٓخِرِينَ ٨٤ وَٱجۡعَلۡنِي مِن وَرَثَةِ جَنَّةِ ٱلنَّعِيمِ﴾

[الشعراء: ٨٣-٨٥]

Rabbi hab lī ḥukmān wa alḥiqnī bil-ṣāliḥīna wa ij'al lī lisāna ṣidqin fī al-ākhirīna wa ij'alnī min warathati jannati al-na'īm.[60]

﴿رَبِّ أَوۡزِعۡنِيٓ أَنۡ أَشۡكُرَ نِعۡمَتَكَ ٱلَّتِيٓ أَنۡعَمۡتَ عَلَيَّ وَعَلَىٰ وَٰلِدَيَّ وَأَنۡ أَعۡمَلَ صَٰلِحٗا تَرۡضَىٰهُ وَأَدۡخِلۡنِي بِرَحۡمَتِكَ فِي عِبَادِكَ ٱلصَّٰلِحِينَ﴾

[النمل: ١٩]

Rabbi awzi'nī an ashkura ni'mataka allatī an'amta 'alayya wa 'alā wālidayya wa an a'mala ṣāliḥan tarḍāhu wa adkhilnī bi-raḥmatika fī 'ibādika al-ṣāliḥīna.[61]

﴿رَبِّ إِنِّي لِمَآ أَنزَلۡتَ إِلَيَّ مِنۡ خَيۡرٖ فَقِيرٞ﴾

[القصص: ٢٤]

Rabbi innī limā anzalta ilayya min khayrin faqīr.[62]

﴿رَبَّنَا وَسِعۡتَ كُلَّ شَيۡءٖ رَّحۡمَةٗ وَعِلۡمٗا فَٱغۡفِرۡ لِلَّذِينَ تَابُواْ وَٱتَّبَعُواْ سَبِيلَكَ وَقِهِمۡ عَذَابَ ٱلۡجَحِيمِ ٧ رَبَّنَا وَأَدۡخِلۡهُمۡ جَنَّٰتِ عَدۡنٍ ٱلَّتِي وَعَدتَّهُمۡ وَمَن صَلَحَ مِنۡ ءَابَآئِهِمۡ وَأَزۡوَٰجِهِمۡ وَذُرِّيَّٰتِهِمۡۚ إِنَّكَ أَنتَ ٱلۡعَزِيزُ ٱلۡحَكِيمُ ٨ وَقِهِمُ ٱلسَّيِّـَٔاتِۚ وَمَن تَقِ ٱلسَّيِّـَٔاتِ يَوۡمَئِذٖ فَقَدۡ رَحِمۡتَهُۥۚ وَذَٰلِكَ هُوَ ٱلۡفَوۡزُ ٱلۡعَظِيمُ﴾

[غافر: ٧-٩]

---

60 My Lord, grant me wisdom and join me with the righteous. And grant me a reputation of honor among later generations. And place me among the inheritors of the Garden of Pleasure. [Quran 26:83-85]

61 My Lord, enable me to be grateful for Your favor which You have bestowed upon me and upon my parents and to do righteousness of which You approve. And admit me, by Your mercy, into [the ranks of] Your righteous servants. [Quran 27:19]

62 My Lord, indeed I am, for whatever good You would send down to me, in need. [Quran 28:24]

Rabbana wasi'ta kulla shay'in raḥmatan wa 'ilman faghfir lilladhīna tābū wa ittaba'ū sabīlaka wa qihim 'adhāba al-jaḥīm. Rabbana wa adkhilhum jannāti 'adnin allatī wa'adtahum wa man ṣalaha min ābā'ihim wa azwājihim wa dhurriyyātihim. Innaka anta al-'azīzu al-ḥakīm. Wa qihimu al-sayyi'āt. Wa man taqi al-sayyi'āti yawma'idhin faqad raḥimtahu wa dhālika huwa al-fawzu al-'aẓīm.[63]

﴿رَّبَّنَا ٱكۡشِفۡ عَنَّا ٱلۡعَذَابَ إِنَّا مُؤۡمِنُونَ﴾

[الدخان: ١٢]

Rabbana ikhshif 'anna al-'adhāba innā mu'minūna.[64]

---

63 Our Lord, You have encompassed all things in mercy and knowledge, so forgive those who have repented and followed Your way and protect them from the punishment of Hellfire. Our Lord, admit them to gardens of perpetual residence which You have promised them and whoever was righteous among their fathers, their spouses and their offspring. Indeed, it is You who is the Exalted in Might, the Wise. And protect them from the evil consequences [of their deeds]. And he whom You protect from evil consequences that Day - You will have given him mercy. And that is the great attainment. [Quran 40:7-9]

64 Our Lord, remove from us the punishment; indeed, we are believers. [Quran 44:12]

Chapter 10

THE *WIRD* WITH MAQĀSID

بِسْمِ اللَّهِ الرَّحْمَٰنِ الرَّحِيمِ ﴿١﴾ الْحَمْدُ لِلَّهِ رَبِّ الْعَالَمِينَ ﴿٢﴾ الرَّحْمَٰنِ الرَّحِيمِ ﴿٣﴾ مَالِكِ يَوْمِ الدِّينِ ﴿٤﴾ إِيَّاكَ نَعْبُدُ وَإِيَّاكَ نَسْتَعِينُ ﴿٥﴾ اهْدِنَا الصِّرَاطَ الْمُسْتَقِيمَ ﴿٦﴾ صِرَاطَ الَّذِينَ أَنْعَمْتَ عَلَيْهِمْ غَيْرِ الْمَغْضُوبِ عَلَيْهِمْ وَلَا الضَّالِّينَ ﴿٧﴾ آمين

اللّٰهُمَّ صَلِّ وَسَلِّمْ عَلَىٰ سَيِّدِنَا مُحَمَّدٍ الفَاتِحِ لِمَا أُغْلِقَ والخَاتِمِ لِمَا سَبَقَ نَاصِرِ الحَقِّ بِالحَقِّ والهَادِى إِلَىٰ صِراطِكَ المُسْتَقِيمِ وعَلَىٰ آلِهِ حَقَّ قَدْرِكَ وَمِقْدَارِكَ العَظِيمِ

سُبْحَانَ رَبِّكَ رَبِّ الْعِزَّةِ عَمَّا يَصِفُونَ ۝ وَسَلَامٌ عَلَى الْمُرْسَلِينَ ۝ وَالْحَمْدُ للهِ رَبِّ الْعَالَمِينَ ۝

أَسْتَغْفِرُ اللّٰه

(100x)

اللّٰهُمَّ صَلِّ وَسَلِّمْ عَلَىٰ سَيِّدِنَا مُحَمَّدٍ الفَاتِحِ لِمَا أُغْلِقَ والخَاتِمِ لِمَا سَبَقَ نَاصِرِ الحَقِّ بِالحَقِّ والهَادِى إِلَىٰ صِراطِكَ المُسْتَقِيمِ وعَلَىٰ آلِهِ حَقَّ قَدْرِكَ

وَمِقْدَارِكَ الْعَظِيمِ

(100x)

سُبْحَانَ رَبِّكَ رَبِّ الْعِزَّةِ عَمَّا يَصِفُونَ ۝ وَسَلَامٌ عَلَى الْمُرْسَلِينَ ۝
وَالْحَمْدُ لِلَّهِ رَبِّ الْعَالَمِينَ ۝

لَا إِلَهَ إِلَّا اللَّه

(100x)

سَيِّدِنَا مُحَمَّدٌ رَسُولُ اللهِ ۝ عَلَيْهِ سَلَامُ اللهِ

إِنَّ اللَّهَ وَمَلَائِكَتَهُ يُصَلُّونَ عَلَى النَّبِيِّ ۚ يَا أَيُّهَا الَّذِينَ آمَنُوا صَلُّوا عَلَيْهِ
وَسَلِّمُوا تَسْلِيمًا

بِسْمِ اللَّهِ الرَّحْمَٰنِ الرَّحِيمِ ۝١ الْحَمْدُ لِلَّهِ رَبِّ الْعَالَمِينَ ۝٢ الرَّحْمَٰنِ
الرَّحِيمِ ۝٣ مَالِكِ يَوْمِ الدِّينِ ۝٤ إِيَّاكَ نَعْبُدُ وَإِيَّاكَ نَسْتَعِينُ ۝٥ اهْدِنَا
الصِّرَاطَ الْمُسْتَقِيمَ ۝٦ صِرَاطَ الَّذِينَ أَنْعَمْتَ عَلَيْهِمْ غَيْرِ الْمَغْضُوبِ
عَلَيْهِمْ وَلَا الضَّالِّينَ ۝٧ آمِين

سُبْحَانَ رَبِّكَ رَبِّ الْعِزَّةِ عَمَّا يَصِفُونَ ۝ وَسَلَامٌ عَلَى الْمُرْسَلِينَ ۝
وَالْحَمْدُ لِلَّهِ رَبِّ الْعَالَمِينَ ۝

إِنَّ اللَّهَ وَمَلَائِكَتَهُ يُصَلُّونَ عَلَى النَّبِيِّ ۚ يَا أَيُّهَا الَّذِينَ آمَنُوا صَلُّوا عَلَيْهِ
وَسَلِّمُوا تَسْلِيمًا

bismillāhir-raḥmānir-raḥīmil-ḥamdu lillāhi rabbil-ʿālamīn, ar-raḥmānir-raḥīm, māliki yawmid-dīn. iyyāka naʿbudu wa iyyāka nastaʿīn. ihdinaṣ-ṣirāṭal-mustaqīm, ṣirāṭal-ladhīna an'amta 'alayhim, ghayril-maghḍūbi 'alayhim wa laḍ-ḍālīn. āmīn.

Allāhumma ṣalli wa sallim 'alā sayyidinā muḥammad-inil-fātiḥi limā ughliqa, wal-khātimi limā sabaqa, nāṣiril-ḥaqqi bil-haqqi, wal-hādī ilā ṣirāṭikal-mustaqīm, wa 'alā ālihi haqqa qadrika wa miqdārikal-'aẓīm.

subḥāna rabbika rabbil-'izzati 'ammā yaṣifūn, wa salāmun 'alal-mursalīn, wal-ḥamdu lillāhi rabbil-'ālamīn.

astaghfirullāh (100x)

Allāhumma ṣalli wa sallim 'alā sayyidinā muḥammad-inil-fātiḥi limā ughliqa, wal-khātimi limā sabaqa, nāṣiril-ḥaqqi bil-haqqi, wal-hādī ilā ṣirāṭikal-mustaqīm, wa 'alā ālihi haqqa qadrika wa miqdārikal-'aẓīm (100x)

subḥāna rabbika rabbil-'izzati 'ammā yaṣifūn, wa salāmun 'alal-mursalīn, wal-ḥamdu lillāhi rabbil-'ālamīn

lā ilāha illa Llāh (100x)

sayyidunā muḥammadur-rasūlul-lāh, 'alayhi salāmul-lāh

inna-llāha wa malā'ikatahu yuṣallūna 'alan-nabiyy. yā ayyu-hal-ladhīna āmanū ṣallū 'alayhi wa sallimū taslīmā

(make personal du'ā')

bismillāhir-raḥmānir-raḥīmil-ḥamdu lillāhi rabbil-'ālamīn, ar-raḥmānir-raḥīm, māliki yawmid-dīn. iyyāka na'budu wa iyyāka nasta'īn. ihdinaṣ-ṣirāṭal-mustaqīm, ṣirāṭal-ladhīna an'amta 'alayhim, ghayril-maghḍūbi 'alayhim wa laḍ-ḍālīn. āmīn.

subḥāna rabbika rabbil-'izzati 'ammā yaṣifūn, wa salāmun 'alal-mursalīn, wal-ḥamdu lillāhi rabbil-'ālamīn

inna-llāha wa malā'ikatahu yuṣallūna 'alan-nabiyy. yā ayyuhal-ladhīna āmanū ṣallū 'alayhi wa sallimū taslīmā

Chapter 11

THE COMPLETE *WAẒĪFAH* WITH MAQĀSID

أَعُوذُ بِاللهِ مِنَ الشَّيْطَانِ الرَّجِيم

(once)

بِسْمِ اللَّهِ الرَّحْمَٰنِ الرَّحِيمِ ﴿١﴾ الْحَمْدُ لِلَّهِ رَبِّ الْعَالَمِينَ ﴿٢﴾ الرَّحْمَٰنِ
الرَّحِيمِ ﴿٣﴾ مَالِكِ يَوْمِ الدِّينِ ﴿٤﴾ إِيَّاكَ نَعْبُدُ وَإِيَّاكَ نَسْتَعِينُ ﴿٥﴾ اهْدِنَا
الصِّرَاطَ الْمُسْتَقِيمَ ﴿٦﴾ صِرَاطَ الَّذِينَ أَنْعَمْتَ عَلَيْهِمْ غَيْرِ الْمَغْضُوبِ
عَلَيْهِمْ وَلَا الضَّالِّينَ ﴿٧﴾ آمِين

(once)

اللّٰهُمَّ صَلِّ وَسَلِّمْ عَلَىٰ سَيِّدِنَا مُحَمَّدٍ الفَاتِحِ لِماَ أُغْلِقَ والخَاتِمِ لِمَا سَبَقَ
نَاصِرِ الحَقِّ بِالحَقِّ والهَادِي إِلَىٰ صِراطِكَ المُسْتَقِيمِ وعَلَىٰ آلِهِ حق قدرِكَ
وَمِقْدَارِكَ العَظِيم

(once)

سُبْحَانَ رَبِّكَ رَبِّ الْعِزَّةِ عَمَّا يَصِفُونَ ﴿١٨٠﴾ وَسَلَامٌ عَلَى الْمُرْسَلِينَ ﴿١٨١﴾
وَالْحَمْدُ لِلَّهِ رَبِّ الْعَالَمِينَ ﴿١٨٢﴾

(once)

أَسْتَغْفِرُ اللهَ العَظِيمَ الَّذي لا إِلٰه إِلَّا هُوَ الْحَيَّ الْقَيُّومَ (وَأَتُوبُ إِلَيْهِ)

(30 times or, for ease, one can say it 10 times with the words in parenthesis added)

اللّٰهُمَّ صَلِّ وَسَلِّمْ عَلَىٰ سَيِّدِنَا مُحَمَّدٍ الفَاتِحِ لِمَا أُغْلِقَ والخَاتِمِ لِمَا سَبَقَ
نَاصِرِ الحَقِّ بِالحَقِّ والهَادِي إِلَىٰ صِراطِكَ المُسْتَقِيمِ وعَلَىٰ آلِهِ حق قَدْرِكَ
وَمِقْدَارِكَ العَظِيم

(50 times or 20 times)

سُبْحَانَ رَبِّكَ رَبِّ الْعِزَّةِ عَمَّا يَصِفُونَ ﴿١٨٠﴾ وَسَلَامٌ عَلَى الْمُرْسَلِينَ ﴿١٨١﴾
وَالْحَمْدُ لِلَّهِ رَبِّ الْعَالَمِينَ ﴿١٨٢﴾

(once)

لَا إِلٰه إِلَّا الله

(100 times or 50 times)

سَيِّدِنَا مُحَمَّدٌ رَسُولُ اللهِ عَلَيْهِ سَلَامُ اللهِ

(once)

اللّٰهُمَّ صَلِّ وَسَلِّمْ عَلَى عَيْنِ الرَّحْمَةِ الرَّبَّانِيَّة وَالْيَاقُوتَةِ الْمُتَحَقِّقَةِ الْحَائِطَةِ بِمَرْكَزِ الْفُهُومِ وَالْمَعَانِي وَنُورِ الْأَكْوَانِ الْمُتَكَوِّنَةِ الْآدَمِيِّ صَاحِبِ الْحَقِّ الرَّبَّانِي الْبَرْقِ الْأَسْطَعِ بِمُزَوِّنِ الْأَرْبَاحِ الْمَالِئَةِ لِكُلِّ مُتَعَرِّضٍ مِنَ الْبُحُورِ وَالْأَوَانِي وَنُورِكَ اللَّامِعِ الَّذِي مَلَأْتَ بِهِ كَوْنَكَ الْمَكْنُونِ فِي السَّبْعِ الْمَثَانِي. اللّٰهُمَّ صَلِّ وَسَلِّمْ عَلَى عَيْنِ الْحَقِّ الَّتِي تَتَجَلَّى مِنْهَا عُرُوش الْحَقَائِقِ عَيْنِ الْمَعَارِفِ الْأَكْرَمِ صِرَاطِكَ التَّامِّ الْأَقْوَمِ اللّٰهُمَّ صَلِّ وَسَلِّمْ عَلَى طَلْعَةِ الْحَقِّ بِالْحَقِّ الْكَنْزِ الْأَعْظَمِ إِفَاضَتِكَ مِنْكَ إِلَيْكَ إِحَاطَةِ النُّورِ الْمُطَلْسَمِ صَلَّى اللهُ عَلَيْهِ وَعَلَى آلِهِ صَلاَةً تُعَرِّفُنَا بِهَا إِيَّاهُ

(11 times or 7 times; if reciting 11 times, it is customary to recite it an additional 12th time as a gift to the presence of the most noble Messenger ﷺ)

إِنَّ اللهَ وَمَلَائِكَتَهُ يُصَلُّونَ عَلَى النَّبِيِّ يَا أَيُّهَا الَّذِينَ آمَنُوا صَلُّوا عَلَيْهِ وَسَلِّمُوا تَسْلِيمًا

(once)

سُبْحَانَ رَبِّكَ رَبِّ الْعِزَّةِ عَمَّا يَصِفُونَ ﴿١٨٠﴾ وَسَلَامٌ عَلَى الْمُرْسَلِينَ ﴿١٨١﴾
وَالْحَمْدُ لِلّٰهِ رَبِّ الْعَالَمِينَ ﴿١٨٢﴾

(once)

-

Transliteration

Aʿūdhu billāhi mina sh-shayṭāni r-rajīm
(once)

bismillāhir-raḥmānir-raḥīmil-ḥamdu lillāhi rabbil-ʿālamīn, ar-raḥmānir-raḥīm, māliki yawmid-dīn. iyyāka naʿbudu wa iyyāka nastaʿīn. ihdinaṣ-ṣirāṭal-mustaqīm, ṣirāṭal-ladhīna anʿamta ʿalayhim, ghayril-maghḍūbi ʿalayhim wa laḍ-ḍālīn. āmīn.
(once)

Allāhumma ṣalli wa sallim ʿalā sayyidinā muḥammad-inil-fātiḥi limā ughliqa, wal-khātimi limā sabaqa, nāṣiril-ḥaqqi bil-haqqi, wal-hādī ilā ṣirāṭikal-mustaqīm, wa ʿalā ālihi haqqa qadrika wa miqdārikal-ʿaẓīm.

(once)

subḥāna rabbika rabbil-ʿizzati ʿammā yaṣifūn, wa salāmun ʿalal-mursalīn, wal-ḥamdu lillāhi rabbil-ʿālamīn

(once)

astaghfiru Llāha l-ʿAdhīma lladhī lā ilāha illā huwa l-Ḥayya l-Qayyūma (wa atūbu ilayh)

(30 times or, for ease, one can say it 10 times with the words in parenthesis added)

Allāhumma ṣalli wa sallim ʿalā sayyidinā muḥammad-inil-fātiḥi limā ughliqa, wal-khātimi limā sabaqa, nāṣiril-ḥaqqi bil-haqqi, wal-hādī ilā ṣirāṭikal-mustaqīm, wa ʿalā ālihi haqqa qadrika wa miqdārikal-ʿaẓīm.

(50 times or 20 times)

subḥāna rabbika rabbil-ʿizzati ʿammā yaṣifūn, wa salāmun ʿalal-mursalīn, wal-ḥamdu lillāhi rabbil-ʿālamīn

(once)

lā ilāha illa Llāh
(100 times or 50 times)

sayyidunā muḥammadur-rasūlul-lāh, ʿalayhi salāmul-lāh

(once)

Allāhumma ṣalli wa sallim ʿalā ʿayni r-raḥmati r-rabbāniyyati wa l-yāqūtati l-mutaḥaqqiqati l-ḥāʾiṭati bi markazi l-fuhūmi wa l-maʿānī wa nūri l-akwāni l-mutakawwinati l-ādamiyyi ṣāḥibi l-ḥaqqi r-rabbānī al-barqi l-asṭaʿi bi muzūni l-arbāḥi l-māliʾati li kulli mutaʿarriḍin mina l-buḥūri wa l-awānī wa nūrika l-lāmiʾ l-ladhī malaʾta bihi kawnaka l-maknūni fi s-sabʿi l-mathānī. Allāhumma ṣalli wa sallim ʿalā ʿayni l-ḥaqqi llatī tatajallā minhā ʿurūshu l-ḥaqāʾiq ʿayni l-maʿārifi l-akram ṣirāṭika t-tāmmi l-aqwam. Allāhumma ṣalli wa sallim ʿalā ṭalʿati l-ḥaqqi bi l-ḥaqqi l-kanzi l-aʿẓam ifāḍatika minka ilayka iḥāṭati n-nūri l-muṭalsam Ṣalla Llāhu ʿalayhi wa ʿalā ālihi ṣalātan tuʿarrifunā bihā iyyāh

(11 times or 7 times; if reciting 11 times, it is customary to recite it an additional 12th time as a gift to the presence of the most noble Messenger ﷺ)

inna-llāha wa malāʾikatahu yuṣallūna ʿalan-nabiyy. yā ayyuhal-ladhīna āmanū ṣallū ʿalayhi wa sallimū taslīmā

(once)

subḥāna rabbika rabbil-ʿizzati ʿammā yaṣifūn, wa salāmun ʿalal-mursalīn, wal-ḥamdu lillāhi rabbil-ʿālamīn

(once)

Chapter 12

THE LITANY OF LOVE

The scholars and knowers are in agreement that the Blessed Quran is the most noble *dhikr*, the most sincere *du'ā'*, and the most eloquent of speech. The *dhikr* and *du'ā'* of the blessedly pure sunnah comes from the same niche. Allah the Exalted has expressly mentioned to His noble Messenger ﷺ and to all the believers to make much *dhikr*: "O you who believe make much remembrance of Allah." And He also exhorted us to make *du'ā'*: "And your Lord said, 'Ask and I will respond to you.'"

The believer is not only allowed to, but is commanded by the Book and Sunnah to do this. Thus, the believer has a clearly valid permission which is not in need of anyone else's permission. Moreover, whoever claims that there is a *dhikr* or *du'ā'* or hizb that is better than or equal to what is contained in the Quran and Sunnah, in terms of excellence or reward, has missed the mark.

His Eminence the Imam has gifted us with the following hizb called "The Litany of Love" (*Ḥizb al-Ḥubb*) containing his eminence's selections of beautiful *dhikr* and great *du'ā'* from the Quran and Sunnah. It should be recited once a day, but if one cannot do that then one should recite it to the extent of one's ability. It has no condition other than love and can be recited in any state and at any time, and it can be repeated any number of times if one wishes. May Allah accept from us and you.

اللّٰهُمَّ إِنَّا نَسْأَلُكَ يَا ذَا الْجَلَالِ وَالْإِكْرَامِ وَيَا ذَا الطَّوْلِ وَالْإِنْعَامِ وَيَا مَنْ أَظْهَرَ الْجَمِيلَ وَسَتَرَ الْقَبِيحَ وَلَمْ يُؤَاخِذْ بِالْجَرِيرَةِ وَلَمْ يَهْتِكِ السِّتْرَ وَيَا عَظِيمَ الْعَفْوِ وَيَا حَسَنَ التَّجَاوُزِ وَيَا وَاسِعَ الْمَغْفِرَةِ وَيَا بَاسِطَ الْيَدَيْنِ بِالرَّحْمَةِ وَيَا سَامِعَ كُلِّ نَجْوَى وَيَا مُنْتَهَى كُلِّ شَكْوَى وَيَا كَرِيمَ الصَّفْحِ وَيَا عَظِيمَ الْمَنِّ وَيَا مُقِيلَ الْعَثَرَاتِ وَيَا مُبْتَدِئًا بِالنِّعَمِ قَبْلَ اسْتِحْقَاقِهَا يَا رَبِّي وَيَا سَيِّدِي وَيَا مَوْلَايَ وَيَا غَايَةَ رَغْبَتِي أَسْأَلُكَ أَلاَّ تُشَوِّهَ خِلْقَتِي بِبَلَاءِ الدُّنْيَا وَلاَ بِعَذَابِ النَّارِ

سُبْحَانَ اللهِ وَبِحَمْدِهِ عَدَدَ خَلْقِهِ وَرِضَاءَ نَفْسِهِ وَزِنَةَ عَرْشِهِ وَمِدَادَ كَلِمَاتِهِ

سُبْحَانَ اللهِ وَبِحَمْدِهِ سُبْحَانَ اللهِ الْعَظِيمِ

سُبْحَانَ اللهِ وَالْحَمْدُ للهِ وَلَا إِلٰـهَ إِلَّا اللهُ وَاللهُ أَكْبَرُ وَلَا حَوْلَ وَلَا قُوَّةَ إِلَّا بِاللهِ حَسْبُنَا اللهُ وَنِعْمَ الْوَكِيلُ

اللّٰهُمَّ اهْدِنَا الصِّرَاطَ الْمُسْتَقِيمَ صِرَاطَ الَّذِينَ أَنْعَمْتَ عَلَيْهِمْ غَيْرِ الْمَغْضُوبِ عَلَيْهِمْ وَ لاَ الضَّالِّينَ

رَبَّنَا آتِنَا فِي الدُّنْيَا حَسَنَةً وَفِي الآخِرَةِ حَسَنَةً وَقِنَا عَذَابَ النَّارِ

رَبَّنَا لاَ تُؤَاخِذْنَا إِن نَّسِينَا أَوْ أَخْطَأْنَا رَبَّنَا وَلاَ تَحْمِلْ عَلَيْنَا إِصْرًا كَمَا حَمَلْتَهُ عَلَى الَّذِينَ مِن قَبْلِنَا رَبَّنَا وَلاَ تُحَمِّلْنَا مَا لاَ طَاقَةَ لَنَا بِهِ وَاعْفُ عَنَّا

وَاغْفِرْ لَنَا وَارْحَمْنَا أَنتَ مَوْلاَنَا فَانصُرْنَا عَلَى الْقَوْمِ الْكَافِرِينَ

رَبَّنَا لاَ تُزِغْ قُلُوبَنَا بَعْدَ إِذْ هَدَيْتَنَا وَهَبْ لَنَا مِن لَّدُنكَ رَحْمَةً إِنَّكَ أَنتَ الْوَهَّابُ

رَبَّنَا آمَنَّا بِمَا أَنزَلْتَ وَاتَّبَعْنَا الرَّسُولَ فَاكْتُبْنَا مَعَ الشَّاهِدِينَ

رَبَّنَا إِنَّنَا سَمِعْنَا مُنَادِيًا يُنَادِي لِلإِيمَانِ أَنْ آمِنُوا بِرَبِّكُمْ فَآمَنَّا رَبَّنَا فَاغْفِرْ لَنَا ذُنُوبَنَا وَكَفِّرْ عَنَّا سَيِّئَاتِنَا وَتَوَفَّنَا مَعَ الأَبْرَارِ

رَبَّنَا وَآتِنَا مَا وَعَدتَّنَا عَلَى رُسُلِكَ وَلاَ تُخْزِنَا يَوْمَ الْقِيَامَةِ إِنَّكَ لاَ تُخْلِفُ الْمِيعَادَ

رَبِّ اجْعَلْنِي مُقِيمَ الصَّلاةِ وَمِن ذُرِّيَّتِي رَبَّنَا وَتَقَبَّلْ دُعَاء

رَبَّنَا اغْفِرْ لِي وَلِوَالِدَيَّ وَلِلْمُؤْمِنِينَ يَوْمَ يَقُومُ الْحِسَابُ

رَبِّ ادْخِلْنِي مُدْخَلَ صِدْقٍ وَأَخْرِجْنِي مُخْرَجَ صِدْقٍ وَاجْعَل لِّي مِن لَّدُنكَ سُلْطَانًا نَّصِيرًا

رَبَّنَا آتِنَا مِن لَّدُنكَ رَحْمَةً وَهَيِّئْ لَنَا مِنْ أَمْرِنَا رَشَدًا

رَبِّ اشْرَحْ لِي صَدْرِي وَيَسِّرْ لِي أَمْرِي وَاحْلُلْ عُقْدَةً مِّن لِّسَانِي يَفْقَهُوا قَوْلِي

رَبِّ اغْفِرْ وَارْحَمْ وَأَنتَ خَيْرُ الرَّاحِمِينَ

رَبَّنَا هَبْ لَنَا مِنْ أَزْوَاجِنَا وَذُرِّيَّاتِنَا قُرَّةَ أَعْيُنٍ وَاجْعَلْنَا لِلْمُتَّقِينَ إِمَامًا

رَبِّ أَوْزِعْنِي أَنْ أَشْكُرَ نِعْمَتَكَ الَّتِي أَنْعَمْتَ عَلَيَّ وَعَلَى وَالِدَيَّ وَأَنْ أَعْمَلَ صَالِحًا تَرْضَاهُ وَأَدْخِلْنِي بِرَحْمَتِكَ فِي عِبَادِكَ الصَّالِحِينَ

اللّٰهُمَّ مَا أَصْبَحَ (أَمْسَى) بِنَا مِنْ نِعْمَةٍ أَوْ بِأَحَدٍ مِّنْ خَلْقِكَ فَمِنْكَ وَحْدَكَ لا شَرِيكَ لَكَ فَلَكَ الْحَمْدُ وَلَكَ الشُّكْرُ

اللّٰهُمَّ صَلِّ عَلَى سَيِّدِنَا مُحَمَّدٍ وَعَلَى آلِ سَيِّدِنَا مُحَمَّدٍ كَمَا صَلَّيْتَ عَلَى سَيِّدِنَا إِبْرَاهِيمَ وَعَلَى آلِ سَيِّدِنَا إِبْرَاهِيمَ فِي الْعَالَمِينَ إِنَّكَ حَمِيدٌ مَّجِيدٌ

السَّلَامُ عَلَيْكَ أَيُّهَا النَّبِيُّ وَرَحْمَةُ اللهِ وَبَرَكَاتُهُ

السَّلَامُ عَلَيْنَا وَ عَلَى عِبَادِ اللهِ الصَّالِحِينَ

رَضِينَا بِاللهِ رَبًّا وَبِالإِسْلَامِ دِينًا وَبِسَيِّدِنَا

مُحَمَّدٍ صَلَّى اللهُ عَلَيْهِ وَسَلَّمَ نَبِيًّا وَرَسُولًا

اللّٰهُمَّ أَنتَ رَبِّي لا إِلٰهَ إِلاَّ أَنتَ خَلَقْتَنِي وَأَنَا عَبْدُكَ وَأَنَا عَلَى عَهْدِكَ وَوَعْدِكَ مَا اسْتَطَعْتُ أَعُوذُ بِكَ مِن شَرِّ مَا صَنَعْتُ أَبُوءُ لَكَ بِنِعْمَتِكَ عَلَيَّ وَأَبُوءُ لَكَ بِذَنْبِي فَاغْفِرْ لِي فَإِنَّهُ لا يَغْفِرُ الذُّنُوبَ إِلاَّ أَنتَ

اللّٰهُمَّ اغْفِرْ لِآبَائِنَا وَأُمَّهَاتِنَا وَمَشَايِخِنَا وَمَن لَّهُ حَقٌّ عَلَيْنَا وَإِخْوَانِنَا وَاجْعَلْهُمْ جَمِيعًا فِي أَعْلَى عِلِيِّينَ مَعَ النَّبِيِّينَ وَالصِّدِّيقِينَ وَالشُّهَدَاءِ وَالصَّالِحِينَ وَحَسُنَ أُولَئِكَ رَفِيقًا

اللّٰهُمَّ اغْفِرْ لِلْمُسْلِمِينَ وَالْمُسْلِمَاتِ وَالْمُؤْمِنِينَ وَالْمُؤْمِنَاتِ الأَحْيَاء مِنْهُمْ وَالأَمْوَاتِ

اللّٰهُمَّ ارْزُقْنَا جَمِيعًا عِلْمًا نَافِعًا وَرِزْقًا وَاسِعًا وَشِفَاء مِن كُلِّ دَاءٍ

اللّٰهُمَّ إِنِّي أَعُوذُ بِوَجْهِكَ الْكَرِيمِ وَبِاسْمِكَ الأَعْظَمِ وَسُلْطَانِكَ الْقَدِيمِ

مِنْ عِلْمٍ لا يُنْفَعُ وَعَمَلٍ لا يُرْفَعُ وَدُعَاءٍ لا يُسْمَعُ وَقَلْبٍ لا يَخْشَعُ وَنَفْسٍ لا تَشْبَعُ

وَأَعُوذُ بِكَ مِنَ الْعَجْزِ وَالْكَسَلِ وَالْهَمِّ وَالْحُزْنِ وَالْجُبْنِ وَالْبُخْلِ وَغَلَبَةِ الدَّيْنِ وَقَهْرِ الرِّجَالِ

وَأَعُوذُ بِكَ مِنَ الْفَقْرِ وَالْكُفْرِ وَالْفُسُوقِ وَالشِّقَاقِ وَالنِّفَاقِ وَسُوءِ الْأَخْلَاقِ

اللّٰهُمَّ إِنِّي أَعُوذُ بِرِضَاكَ مِنْ سَخَطِكَ وَبِمَعَافَاتِكَ مِنْ عُقُوبَتِكَ وَأَعُوذُ بِكَ مِنكَ لا أُحْصِي ثَنَاءً عَلَيْكَ أَنْتَ كَمَا أَثْنَيْتَ عَلَى نَفْسِكَ

اللّٰهُمَّ إِنِّي أَسْأَلُكَ حُبَّكَ وَ رِضَاكَ وَ رِضْوَانَكَ وَ لَذَّةَ النَّظَرِ إِلَي وَجْهِكَ الْكَرِيمِ وَصُحْبَةَ رَسُولِكَ الْعَظِيمِ فِي أَعْلَي عِلِّيِّينَ

اللّٰهُمَّ إِنِّي أَسْأَلُكَ مِنَ الْخَيْرِ كُلِّهِ مَا عَلِمْتُ مِنْهُ وَمَا لَمْ أَعْلَمْ

وَأَعُوذُ بِكَ مِنَ الشَّرِّ كُلِّهِ مَا عَلِمْتُ مِنْهُ وَمَا لَمْ أَعْلَم

اللّٰهُمَّ صَلِّ وَسَلِّمْ عَلَى سَيِّدِنَا مُحَمَّدٍ الفَاتِحِ لِمَا أُغْلِقَ وَالْخَاتِمِ لِمَا سَبَقَ نَاصِرِ الْحَقِّ بِالْحَقِّ وَالْهَادِي إِلَى صِرَاطِكَ الْمُسْتَقِيمِ وَعَلَى آلِهِ حَقَّ قَدْرِكَ وَمِقْدَارِكَ الْعَظِيمِ

سُبْحَانَ رَبِّكَ رَبِّ الْعِزَّةِ عَمَّا يَصِفُونَ وَسَلَامٌ عَلَى الْمُرْسَلِينَ وَالْحَمْدُ لِلّٰهِ رَبِّ الْعَالَمِينَ

Allahumma inna nas›aluka ya dha al-jalali wal-ikrami wa ya dha at-tawli wal-in›am, wa ya man adhara al-jamila wa satar al-qabih, wa lam yu›akhidh bil-jarirah, wa lam yahtikis-sitr. Wa ya ‹azima al-›afwi wa ya hasana at-tajawuzi, wa ya wasi›a al-maghfirah, wa ya basita al-yadayni bi ar-rahmah, wa ya sami›a kulli najwa, wa ya muntaha kulli shakwa, wa ya karima as-safh, wa ya ‹azima al-man, wa ya muqila al-›atharat, wa ya mubtadi›an bin-na›mi qabla istihaqihā. Ya Rabbi wa ya Sayyidi wa ya Maulāy wa ya Ghāyata raghbatī, as›aluka allā tushwih khalaqatī bi balā›id-dunyā wa lā bi›athābin-nār.

Subḥānallāhi wa bi-hamdihi ‹adada khalqihi wa riḍā›an nafsihi wa zinata ‹arshihi wa midāda kalimātih.

Subḥānallāhi wa bi-hamdihi Subḥānallāhil-›Azīm.

Subḥānallāhi walḥamdulillāh wa lā ilāha illallāh, wallāhu akbar, wa lā ḥawla wa lā quwwata illā billāh. Ḥasbunallāhu wa ni›mal-wakīl.

Allahumma ihdinā l-ṣirāṭ al-mustaqīm, ṣirāṭ al-ladhīna an›amta ‹alayhim ghayri l-maghḍūbi ‹alayhim walāḍ-ḍāllīn.

Rabbanā ātinā fī d-dunyā ḥasanaẗan wa fī l-ākhirati ḥasanaẗan wa qinā ‹adhāba n-nār.

Rabbanā lā tu›ākhidhnā in nasīnā aw akhṭa›nā. Rabbanā walā taḥmil ‹alaynā iṣran kama ḥamaltahu ‹alā l-laḏīna min qablīnā. Rabbanā walā tuḥammi lanā mā lā ṭāqata lanā bih. Waghfir lanā wairḥamnā. Anta Mawlānā fa-nsurnā ‹alā l-qawm al-kāfirīn.

Rabbanā lā tuzigh qulūbanā ba›da idh hadaytanā wa hab lanā min ladunka raḥmatan innaka anta l-Wahhāb.

Rabbanā āmannā bimā anzalta wāttabi›nā r-rasūla fa-ktubnā ma›ash-shāhidīn.

Rabbanā innanā sami›nā munādīan yunādī li-l-īmāni an āminū bi-Rabbikum fa-āmannā, Rabbanā fa-ghfir lanā dhunūbana wa kaffir ‹annā sayyi›ātinā wa tawaffanā ma›aṣ-ṣāliḥīn.

Rabbanā wa ātina mā wa›adtanā ‹alā rusulika walā tu khz i nā yawm al-qiyāmah innaka lā tu kh lifu l-mī›ād.

Rabbi ij›alnī muqīmas-ṣalāti wa min dhurriyyatī, Rabbana wataqabbal du›ā›

Rabbanā ighfirlī wa li-wālidayya wa lil-mu›minīna yawma yaqūm al-ḥisāb. Rabbi adkhilnī mudkhala ṣidqin wa akhrijnī mukhraja ṣidqin wa ij›al lī min ladunka sultaanan naṣīra.

Rabbanā ātina min ladunka raḥmatan wa hayyi› lanā min amrinā rashadā.

Rabbi ishrah lī ṣadrī, wa yassir lī amrī, wāḥlul ‹uqdatan min lisānī, yafqahu qawlī.

Rabbi ighfir warḥam wa anta khayr ar-raḥimīn.

Rabbanā hab lanā min azwājinā wa dhurriyyātinā qurrata ‹ayn, wa ij›alnā lil-muttaqīna imāma.

Rabbi awzhi›nī an ashkur ni›mataka allatī an›amta ‹alayya wa ‹alā wālidayya wa an a›mala ṣāliḥan tarḍahu.

Allāhumma mā aṣbaḥa (amsā) binā min ni'matin aw bi-aḥadin min khalqika fa-minka waḥdaka lā sharīka laka, falaka l-ḥamd wa laka sh-shukr.

Allāhumma ṣalli 'alā sayyidinā Muḥammadin wa 'alā āli sayyidinā Muḥammadin kamā ṣallayta 'alā sayyidinā Ibrāhīma wa 'alā āli sayyidinā Ibrāhīma fī l-'ālamīna innaka ḥamīdun majīd.

As-salāmu 'alayka ayyuhan-nabīyu wa raḥmatu-llāhi wa barakātuhu.

As-salāmu 'alaynā wa 'alā 'ibādillaahi-ṣ-ṣāliḥīn.

Raḍīnā billāhi rabbān wa bil-islāmi dīnan wa bi-sayyidinā Muḥammadin ṣallā Allāhu 'alayhi wa sallam nabiyyan wa rasūlan.

Allāhumma anta rabbi lā ilāha illā anta, khalaqtanī wa anā 'abduka, wa anā 'alā 'ahdika wa wa'dika ma astaṭa'tu, a'ūdhu bika min sharri mā ṣana'tu, abū'u laka bini'matika 'alayya, wa abū'u laka bidhanbī, faghfir lī, fa innahu lā yaghfiru-ẓ-ẓunūba illā anta.

Allāhumma-ghfir li-ābā'ina wa ummahātina, wa mashāyikhinā, wa man lahu ḥaqqun 'alaynā, wa ikhwāninā, waj'alhum jamī'an fī a'lā 'illiyyīn, ma'an-nabīyīna waṣ-ṣiddīqīna wa sh-shuhadā'i wa-ṣ-ṣāliḥīna, wa ḥasuna ulā'ika rafīqā.

Allāhumma-ghfir lil-muslimīna wal-muslimāt, wal-mu'minī-na wal-mu'mināt, al-aḥyā'i minhum wal-amwāt.

Allāhumma-rzuqnā jamī'an 'ilman nāfi'an, wa rizqan wā-si'an, wa shifā'an min kulli dā'in.

Allāhumma innī a'ūdhu bi wajhika l-karīmi, wa bismika l-a'ẓam, wa sulṭānika l-qadīmi min 'ilmin lā yanfa'u, wa 'ama-lin lā yurfā'u, wa du'ā'in lā yusma'u, wa qalbin lā yakhsha'u, wa nafsin lā tashba'u.

Wa a'ūdhu bika min al-ajzi wal-kasal, wa l-hami wa l-ḥazn, wa l-jubni wal-bukhl, wa ghalabati d-dīn, wa qahrir-rijāl.

Wa a'ūdhu bika min al-faqr, wal-kufr, wa l-fusūqi wa sh-shiqāq, wa n-nifāqi wa sūi l-akhlāq.

Allāhumma innī a'ūdhu biraḍāka min sakhaṭika, wa bi-ma'āfātika min 'uqūbatika, wa a'ūdhu bika, lā uḥṣī thanā'an 'alayka, anta kamā 'athnayta 'alā nafsika.

Allāhumma innī as'aluka ḥubbaka wa riḍāka wa riḍāwanaka wa laḍḍata n-nẓẓari ilā wajhika l-karīmi wa ṣaḥbata rasūlika l-'aẓīmi fī a'lā 'illiyyīn.

Allāhumma innī as'aluka mina l-khayri kullihi, mā 'alimtu minhu, wa mā lam a'lam.

Wa a'ūdhu bika mina sh-sharri kullihi, mā 'alimtu minhu, wa mā lam a'lam.

Allāhumma ṣalli 'alā sayyidinā Muḥammad, al-fātiḥi limā ughliqa, wal-khātimi limā sabaqa, nāṣiri l-ḥaqqi bil-ḥaqqi, wal-hādī ilā ṣirāṭika l-mustaqīm, wa 'alā ālih, ḥaqqi qadrika wa miqdārika l-'aẓīm.

Subḥāna rabbika rabbil-'izzati 'ammā yaṣifūna, wa salāmun

'alā l-mur'salīna, wal-ḥamdulillāhi rabbil-'ālamīn.[65]

65 O Allah, we beseech You, O Possessor of Majesty and Generosity, O Possessor of Abundance and Graciousness, O One who reveals beauty and conceals ugliness, who does not take people to account for their unintended mistakes, and who does not strip them of their dignity. O All-Forgiving, O Most Merciful in pardoning, O All-Encompassing in forgiveness, O One who extends His hands with mercy, O All-Hearing of every secret, O One who resolves all complaints, O Most Generous in forgiveness, O All-Magnificent, O Supporter of those who stumble, O Initiator of blessings even before they are deserved.

My Lord, my Master, my Guardian, and the Ultimate Goal of my desires, I implore You not to let the trials of this world or the punishment of the Fire mar my existence. Glory be to Allah, and all praise is due to Him, as numerous as His creations, and as vast as His acceptance. Glory be to Allah, the Almighty. Glory be to Allah, and all thanks are to Him. There is no deity worthy of worship except Allah, and Allah is the Greatest. There is no power or strength except through Allah. Allah is sufficient for us, and He is the best disposer of affairs.

O Allah, guide us to the Straight Path, the path of those whom You have blessed, not the path of those who have earned Your anger nor of those who have gone astray.

Our Lord, grant us good in this world and good in the Hereafter, and save us from the punishment of the Fire.

Our Lord, do not hold us accountable if we forget or make a mistake. Our Lord, do not burden us beyond our strength as You burdened those before us. Our Lord, do not place upon us what we have no ability to bear, and pardon us, forgive us, and have mercy on us. You are our Protector, so grant us victory over the disbelieving people.

Our Lord, do not let our hearts deviate after You have guided us and grant us mercy from Your presence. Indeed, You are the Bestower.

Our Lord, we have believed, so forgive us and have mercy upon us, for You are the Best of the Merciful.

Our Lord, grant us what You promised us through Your messengers and do not disgrace us on the Day of Resurrection. Indeed, You do not fail in [Your] promise.

My Lord, make me steadfast in prayer, and also my descendants. Our

---

Lord, accept my supplication.

My Lord, forgive me, my parents, and the believers on the Day when the account will be established.

My Lord, admit me by Your mercy into [the ranks of] Your righteous servants.

O Allah, whatever blessings came upon us today or upon any of Your creations, are solely from You, and You have no partner. For You is all praise and all gratitude.

O Allah, send blessings upon our Master Muhammad and upon the family of our Master Muhammad, just as You sent blessings upon our Master Ibrahim and upon the family of our Master Ibrahim. Indeed, You are praiseworthy and glorious.

Peace be upon you, O Prophet, and the mercy of Allah and His blessings.

Peace be upon us and upon the righteous servants of Allah.

We are content with Allah as our Lord, with Islam as our religion, and with Muhammad, peace be upon him, as our Prophet and Messenger.

O Allah, I seek Your love, Your pleasure, Your contentment, and the pleasure of looking at Your noble face and being with Your great Messenger in the highest abode of bliss.

O Allah, send blessings upon our Master Muhammad, the opener of what was closed, the seal of what preceded, the supporter of truth with truth, and the guide to Your straight path. And upon his family, according to his esteemed and mighty rank.

Glory be to Your Lord, the Lord of Honor and Power. He is free from what they ascribe [to Him], and peace be upon the messengers. And all praise is due to Allah, the Lord of the worlds.

Chapter 15

صَلاةُ الحُبّ

THE ṢALĀT OF LOVE

اللهم صَلِّ وَسَلِّمْ عَلَى سَيِّدِنَا مُحَمَّدٍ صَلاَةً تُعَرِّفُنَا بِهَا إِيَّاهُ وعَلَى آلِهِ حَقَّ قَدْرِكَ وَمِقْدَارِكَ العَظِيمِ

Allāhumma ṣalli wa sallim ʿalā sayyidinā muḥammadin ṣalātan tuʿarrifunā bihā iyyāhu wa ʿalā ālihi ḥaqqa qadrika wa miqdārikal-ʿaẓīm[66]

This is a prayer that emerged from the fervor of the hidden Pole. It gathers the two prayers, *Jawharat al-Kamāl* and *Ṣalāt al-Fātiḥ* in a single cup. The numerical value of its letters are 66, which - according to the Eastern and Western calculations - is equivalent to the word 'Allah.'

The letter *alif* = 1
The letter *lām* = 30 + 30 (there are two *lāms*)
The letter *hā* = 5

---

66 O Allah, send ṣalāt and salām upon our master Muhammad, a ṣalāt by which you make us know him, and upon his family, as befits Your worth and esteem.

Thus, *alif* + *lām* + *lām* + *hā* = 66

THE ṢALĀT OF LIGHT

اللهم صَلِّ وَسَلِّمْ عَلَى سَيِّدِنَا مُحَمَّدٍ وعَلَى آلِهِ
وَالْمُؤْمِنِينَ وَالْمُؤْمِنَاتِ وَالْمُسْلِمِينَ وَالْمُسْلِمَاتِ

Allāhumma ṣalli wa sallim ʿalā sayyidinā muḥammadin wa ʿalā ālihi wa l-muʾminīna wa l-muʿmināti wa l-muslimīna wa l-muslimāt[67]

This is a great and immense prayer that emerged from the presence of lordly Light. It gathers together verses: "***Verily, Allah and His angels send ṣalāt on the Prophet. O you who believe, send ṣalāt on him and prayers of peace***" and "***He is the One who sends ṣalāt on you [believers] as do His angels that He may bring you out of darknesses into the Light.***"

As such this prayer is called the Prayer of Light. It is narrated from Abū Saʿīd al-Khudrī ﵁ by al-Bukhārī in his *al-Adab al-Mufrid*, and by Ibn Ḥibbān, al-Bayhaqī, and al-Daylamī. He relates that the Messenger of Allah ﷺ said, "If a man has nothing to give as charity, then let him say 'O Allah, send ṣalāt on Muhammad, your servant and messenger, and send ṣalāt on the believing men and women, and the submitting men and women' for it is a zakat.' This is because he or she is giving charity with the prayer for blessings and peace for the believing and submitting men and women after mention of the Messenger of Alah ﷺ and his blessed family.

Its blessings and lights will envelop all of the believing and submitting men and women from the time of Adam to the blowing of the trumpet.

---

67 O Allah, send ṣalāt and salām upon our master Muhammad and upon his family and all the believing and submitting men and women.

The number of its letters is 66 which is the same as the numerical value of the Name of Allah according to the Eastern and Western methods of calculation. Thus, all spiritual wayfaring and spritual attraction is perfected through the two prayers: the Prayer of Light and the Prayer of Love. And praise be to Allah, Lord of the worlds.

We can combine the two prayers of Light and Love, forming a prayer of utter beauty and perfection and this is the Prayer of the Light of Love:

اللهم صَلِّ وَسَلِّمْ عَلَى سَيِّدِنَا مُحَمَّدٍ صَلَاةً تُعَرِّفُنَا بِهَا إِيَّاهُ وَعَلَى آلِهِ
وَالمُؤْمِنِينَ وَالمُؤْمِنَاتِ وَالمُسْلِمِينَ وَالمُسْلِمَاتِ حَقَّ قَدْرِكَ وَمِقْدَارِكَ العَظِيمِ

Allāhumma ṣalli wa sallim ʿalā sayyidinā muḥammadin ṣalātan tuʿarrifunā bihā iyyāhu wa ʿalā ālihi wa l-muʾminīna wa l-muʿmināti wa l-muslimīna wa l-muslimāt ḥaqqa qadrika wa miqdārikal-ʿaẓīm[68]

68 O Allah, send ṣalāt and salām upon our master Muhammad, a ṣalāt by which you make us know him, and upon his family, and upon all the believing and submitting men and women, as befits Your worth and esteem.

www.ingramcontent.com/pod-product-compliance
Ingram Content Group UK Ltd.
Pitfield, Milton Keynes, MK11 3LW, UK
UKHW060400300726
14090UKWH00001B/44

* 9 7 9 8 2 1 8 2 7 8 5 8 8 *